TODAY
and
EVERY DAY

by

Elizabeth Searle Lamb

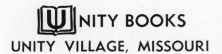

UNITY BOOKS
UNITY VILLAGE, MISSOURI

Foreword

Look to this day, this very day! Celebrate it; fill it with life, the very life of life. Make it a celebration of the Spirit, a singing of the spirit of man tuned to the universal harmonies of Spirit, the infinite Spirit which is the no-beginning/no-ending Source.

Tuned in, sometimes with interference from the busyness of mind or hampered by inability to find the word with which to express the Word, I have celebrated the Spirit with my own spirit, as I was able.

Forget the shape of form, the sound of other singing. Let lack and limitation fade away. Enter into the radiance of joy, the totality of love, the harmony of order, the growth of wisdom. May there be in these pages a word of mine to meet a need of yours. Let us celebrate together that Spirit which is I AM, which is also ALL IS.

E.S.L.

Acknowledgments

For permission to reprint material which first appeared in their pages, grateful acknowledgment is made to the following: Aspire to Better Living, Capper's Weekly, Clear Horizons, Columbus Citizen-Journal, Daily Meditation, The Denver Post, Fellowship Messenger, The Link, The Mennonite, Award Winning Poems 1964: Rochester Festival of Religious Arts, Science of Mind, The Sign, Vision, and War Cry.

"September Praise" originally appeared in The Christian Home, September 1967. Copyright ©1967 by Graded Press.

"Each His Own Explorer" and "Winter Fields" are reprinted by permission from The Christian Science Monitor ©1967, ©1966, The Christian Science Publishing Society. All rights reserved.

Thanks are also due to the publications of Unity: *Daily Word, Good Business, New Magazine, Progress, Weekly Unity,* and *Unity,* in which much of this material was first printed.

CONTENTS

A Celebration of January

A Celebration of February

A Celebration of March

A Celebration of April

A Celebration of May

A Celebration of June

A Celebration of July

A Celebration of August

A Celebration of September

A Celebration of October

A Celebration of November

A Celebration of December

A CELEBRATION OF JANUARY

On January First

Rejoice! Rejoice!
Rejoice in this opening-out new year—
Hope, a blazing sun in an infinite sky.
Rejoice in a multiplying dream—
Faith, immensely deep and sightlessly high.
Rejoice in ever-expanding progress
For which no man can build a gauge.
Rejoice in the opening up of vision—
Now begins a tremendous age!
Rejoice then, oh, rejoice in Truth,
For Truth is world's release
And only this is real:
Truth is Peace!
Believe! Believe! And then
Rejoice!

Credo for a New Year

I believe
that I enter a glorious new year
to be filled with prayer and praise,
with service to God and mankind,
with inspired creative activity.
I believe
that God's presence goes with me
wherever I shall go this year,
by train or bus or car or boat,
slowly paced on foot or high in air.
I believe
His love is shining in my heart,
His life is radiant in my body,
His wisdom guides my mind,
His peace fills me with poise,
His strength is ever at my call.
Oh, I believe
that this is God's new year!

January Resolution

Into the new year I take
The power of prayer to order
My days—indeed, my life—
Into a pattern of progress.

Into the new year I take
The joy of adventuring to lift
The routine into a challenge
Of increasing achievement.

Into the new year I take
The miracle of love to give
As a silent, unseen gift
To each person I meet.

Into the new year I take
Peace at the very center of being,
That it may flow out from me,
Unceasing, till it encompasses the world.

Into the new year I take
God as the fundamental truth
Of all I am, of all I do.
I live in His kingdom forever.

A Spiritual Venture

Venture is "a word with built-in daring." It calls to mind merchants sending their ships to bring home exotic cargoes of silks and spices, the enterprise financed by shares, ventures divided perhaps among family and friends. To venture has had business connotations for generations, with some overtones of risk.

Today there is spiritual venturing to be done. The realm of mind and spirit has not yet been fully explored; even where explored, the benefits have not been fully realized in human lives. Men and women need to venture in this field. They need to risk the small, personal elements of self in the quest for the true Self. Certain material elements must be risked, perhaps, in searching for the enduring values of life.

To venture on a spiritual quest is to set out upon it in a spirit of excitement, of daring, of believing. It is a voyage of discovery in which the objectives cannot be fully plotted at the start. It is an open-minded, open-ended search for answers to the questions of life.

Each one who undertakes such a venture must go alone. He must seek through prayer to make communion with God, to gain understanding of the meaning of life. He must be prepared to sacrifice unnecessary ballast of false beliefs and negative attitudes.

Venture into outer space must now be balanced by inner spiritual venture, undertaken by dedicated men and women.

Each His Own Explorer

There are no maps.

It is a chartless sea he sails
inward to the center of his being
seeking that small island of serenity,
the knowing of oneness.
It is a long but timeless journey
if he fails to find the way;
it is as timeless if he finds his way.
You would think, explorer having found
the place, he would plant a flag there
or bury the mementos of the voyage
beneath a cairn of rocks.
But after the journey all he will say
is, "You must find your own way
across the chartless sea of the self."

There are no maps.

A Prayer in January

Dear Father-God, now as a new year is beginning, I rededicate my life to You. This year I will be more faithful in putting You first. I will pray daily for Your help and guidance, and act upon that guidance more fearlessly. I will give thanks daily for the blessings that surround me.

During this year I will learn to see You more fully as the source of all good, as the answer to each problem whether it be big as an elephant or small as a snail, and as the very real protection surrounding me regardless of whatever danger may at any time come near me.

During this year I will look for new ways to give my tithe to You. I will make a tithe of the money increase that comes to me, yes, but also I will give You this year a tithe of time and talent, a tithe of service.

All of life is an exciting challenge. At the beginning of this new year, I look forward into the unknown, confident that You will be by my side, guiding me into ever fuller use of the abilities and talents You have given me, and sharing my triumphs and achievements.

Dear God, I thank You for a new year filled with unlimited possibilities.

Amen.

Whetstone for Faith

Have you not asked yourself, as I have: "Why did this happen to me? Why was I in this accident or involved in that situation? Why too many bills and not enough ready cash? Why this physical difficulty?"

In the midst of the inner turmoil that a sudden problem brings, it is hard to take the long view, the clear view. It is difficult to believe that any good can come from the situation.

However, life is growth, and growth requires challenge. The manager of a tree farm knows that the straightest, hardest, premium timber logs come from trees that have had to reach up for light and growing space in the midst of close competition. They have had to send their roots down deep to get nourishment. They have had to meet a challenge for survival.

So we should meet the sudden problem by seeing it as a challenge, by knowing that through the meeting of it we shall be sharpening our faith; we shall be growing in wisdom and stature.

Time and energy are wasted in the "Why did this happen to me?" questioning. Problems happen to everyone. The child learning to walk has a problem—he falls down. He doesn't lie on his back wondering why—he tries again! The young student has problems with lessons; the teen-ager faces identity crises. The problems are real ones, but if faced they are eventually conquered. And so, as adults we should forget the "why" and see the problem as a stretching bar to spiritual maturity, and map a course that will lead to a solution.

Faith grows through problems if they are faced

13

with a three-way plan. Prayer, action, and expectation are the three steps that may be applied to any problem, be it health or wealth, inharmonious relationships, or unpleasant situations.

Praying should be the first instinctive act when we come up against a problem stone wall. A sudden emergency? We can pray instantly, silently or aloud. Otherwise, we should take the problem into regular daily meditation and prayer. In deep meditative silence we can lay the problem before God, asking His guidance and remaining receptive to Him, then giving thanks that all will be well—indeed, is well now!

Guidance comes when we ask for it. Sometimes we fail to hear it or be aware of it. We may be too firmly tied to our own idea of a solution. We may fail to be receptive to guidance that comes in an unexpected manner or from a strange source. But guidance does come, and once it does, we must act upon it. We must, (oh, we truly must!) step out with a firm tread to do whatever we are led to do. Such action often takes courage. The way may seem utterly strange; friends and family may be appalled by our action. However, we must do it if we are to reap the growth benefit that lies in meeting the challenge.

Not the least in importance is the third step: expectation. We must expect only good; we must expect a perfect solution; we must expect constantly, without faltering, without giving way to fear or doubt. We must start each day with the joyous hope of healing for the disease, an abundance to fill the lack, a door opening to new and greater good. We must expect nothing but the good, and we most assuredly will receive that good in abundant measure!

14

Looking back, we can see that we have met and overcome certain problems, and that these have never again troubled us. We have grown through these lessons, have come up over them. Now we are faced with a new, a greater challenge. How exciting this is! It means we are making progress through the textbook of life.

As we remain true to God, faithful in prayer communication, developing acute hearing in listening for His guidance, unhesitatingly taking the outer action called for, and unwaveringly expectant, then indeed our faith will be sharpened on the whetstone of life's experience. That faith will be a shining sword clearing the path to the final victory of eternal life.

For All Children

God bless each child
With peace profound;
May dreams be mild
And sleep be sound.
God give to each
Tomorrow's bread
Within his reach;
And give his head
And heart and hands
A job to do
In childhood's lands
(These days are few),
And give him strength,
Dear God, I pray,
Through life's length
To walk Your way.

Work

I start my work for this day by dedicating myself and all that I do to God and to His glory. Whatever I do, I do for Him. Joy springs up in my heart and puts a new glow on my work and on all that I do.

If I am doing work that I love, it is easy for me to put my heart in it, easy to do it perfectly. I look for ways to improve my efficiency and increase my productivity. I look for extra ways to serve, extra ways to give an added blessing.

If I am doing work that is not what my heart desires, work that I have not chosen, I will nevertheless do it to the best of my ability. I will rejoice in having work to do. This enables me to do my work with joy, to give extra, unrequired service.

I hold a dream in my heart of even greater work that I may, that I *will,* one day do to the glory of God. As I work with joy, I am shown steps I can take to be worthy of this greater work, even as I do the work at hand.

I work with joy; my work glorifies God.

Thought-Starters

Does your faith lead you to expect direct, instant answer to prayer?

Do you actually believe prayer can produce worldwide peace?

Given uninterrupted opportunity, how long could you meditate on the presence of God without woolgathering?

Do you use inner meditation to chart outer action?

What percentage of your daily thought production falls into a negative category?

Prayer for Health

Dear Father-God, bless me with perfect health. Your pattern for my growth is one of perfection. I now accept the perfect well-being which is Your will for me and I show forth radiant health and strength in mind and body.

Dear Father-God, bless my mind and the thoughts I think. I now think thoughts of health, of vigor, of steady development. I let go completely of negative thoughts concerning my body. I expect only health to manifest itself within me.

Dear Father-God, bless my lips and the words they speak. Bless my eyes that I may see Your goodness and Your beauty all about me. Bless my ears with perfect hearing that I may hear the underlying harmony of the universe.

Dear Father-God, I ask a blessing for every part of me. I am open to Your radiant life; let it pour through me now, washing away every imperfection until I stand before You, perfectly, radiantly, healthy, and whole.

Amen.

January Is

a new fall of snow
before even a sparrow
has walked down the drive;
a dune of shifting sand
new-swept by the sea breeze;
a fresh letterhead
awaiting first touch
of the pen.

Silence

Be still.
"Be still, and know
That I am God." Alone,
In utter quietness reach out
To Me.

Be still.
The silent hour
Will bring My love to fill
Your need, My wisdom to your quest,
My joy.

Be still.
Reach deep within
To new horizons where
Your soul will find reality.
Be still.

There Will Come

into the dark of night
starshine

into the turmoil of day
an extra measure
of strength

into the hurricane
the eye of calm

into the inner heart
faith

but none of these
are seen
from behind shuttered
windows.

A CELEBRATION OF FEBRUARY

February

The first frail snowdrops
putting out bloom
above the snow;
a blush of palest mauve
appearing long before the green
on eastern mountain slopes;
a robin appearing from nowhere
to peck at frozen apples
in the orchard;
an inner timetable
marks the season's cycle.
Man, too, feels the stir
and looks to new challenge,
prays to God with a fresh joy
even in the midst of blizzard.
God has surely endowed
all living things
with an urge to growth
and a will to achieve fulfillment.

A Psalm for Today

O Lord, I sing a psalm to Thee
Of earth and sky and tide-pulled sea,
A song of rockets, satellites,
Of sonic speeds, unmeasured heights
That man must strip of mystery
The while his inner search must be
A torment gnawing at his soul,
Unrecognized, and unfulfilled
In probe of earth and sky and sea
Until he learns—he seeks but Thee.

Credo for Health

I acknowledge perfect, radiant health as my heritage. I claim my inheritance today.

I begin today to build a new consciousness of health.

I erase from my consciousness all thought of limitation, of disease, and bodily malfunctioning.

I affirm the life and health, the perfection and radiance of every body cell.

I call upon the inner Spirit to direct and superintend the functioning of every cell, tissue, bone, and organ of my body.

I relax in my assurance of perfect health.

I give thanks for the sure, quick manifestation of perfection in my body.

I praise the healing forces at work and give joyous thanks for each manifestation of healing.

I pray for God's blessing on my body and, praying, affirm the instant manifestation of perfection.

I claim, I realize health now, today, this moment.

Thought - Starters

Do you ever procrastinate with prayer?

Can you see the Christ Spirit in a man who cheats you out of a commission you think you earned?

Do you think the omnipresence of God includes the scene of an auto wreck?

Have you ever spiritually oriented yourself for success?

Can you honestly consider your most pressing problem as a challenge to new spiritual growth?

Spiritual Resources

You do not need an oil well to make your dreams come true. You do not need bonds in the bank, or even cash in your purse. . . . Just begin now, wherever you are, to use the spiritual resources that surround you. God, All-Good, *is* the basic spiritual resource. However, as with natural resources, so there are byproducts or individual elements—aspects of this Source—which may be thought of as usable spiritual resources. Divine love, divine guidance, divine power, divine abundance are spiritual resources to be used in mind, body, and affairs through application of faith, prayer, and action.

Divine love is the healing, life-giving resource. Immerse your whole being in it. Let it flood every cell of your body, washing away every imperfection, harmonizing and regulating every part and every function. Let it bring you to a closeness with God so real that you will never again feel loneliness. Silently but consciously send it out to the whole world.

Divine guidance is perhaps the most practical spiritual resource. Seek it; learn to recognize it when it comes; act on it. Do not decide beforehand what you think God wants you to do. Ask, then listen, then follow the guidance you receive. In so doing, you will find the one specific job you were meant to do in life; in doing it you will find yourself, your Christ self.

Divine power is a resource that must accompany the others. It is unlimited! God's strength, His protection are yours when you call upon Him with faith; His power can take you safely through fire, flood, battlefield, hurricane—through *any* experience!

Divine abundance—what does this mean? Simply that there *is* a limitless, inexhaustible supply of everything good. There is enough for every person. When you use this resource you no longer limit your thoughts of supply in quantity, quality, or time. There is abundance now! Claim it; use it; give it. By so doing you complete the circuit of giving and receiving.

Faith, prayer, and action are the techniques of management and utilization of spiritual resources. As you develop these techniques, the spiritual resources you work with will bring more and greater good into your life. You will, indeed, be seeking the kingdom of God first, and all other things will be added.

Faith is simply believing—believing that God is the source of all. Start where you are, with what faith you have. Remember, "If you have faith as a grain of mustard seed, you will say to this mountain, 'move hence to yonder place,' and it will move; and nothing will be impossible to you."

Through prayer you commune with God. Alone, in a quiet place, think of Him. "Our Father who art in heaven . . . " Slowly, deeply, let these words fill your mind and spirit. Let them flow from the very center of your being into the very heart of God, which is both within and without you, the very Source of life. Practice resting in His presence; practice listening. Stay close to God after prayer as well as during prayer.

Then there must be action, based on faith and guided by prayer. Follow guidance fearlessly, unhesitatingly, joyously. So will the self-renewing spiritual resources, increasing as you use them, solve every problem. With the very presence of God active within you, you will attain every dream and meet every challenge victoriously!

A Prayer

Dear God,
Today is my prayer,
Forgetting yesterday
And unaware of tomorrow.
Oh let Your strength
Fill my need;
An inner knowing
Tell Your guidance;
Your peace
As the calm center
Of my being.
Show me the need
You would have me fill
And make me aware
Of You all this day long.

Amen.

Winter Fields

The field lies fallow
after the yield has been gathered,
dirt drifting into the hedgerows.
Sparrows eat fallen seeds
and snow sifts over the furrows.
A young fox passes this way.
At night rabbits play here
in the cold moonlight.
So a man, within himself,
sometimes lies fallow for a season.
Outwardly speaks, is spoken to,
works and plays and loves and sleeps,
yet is dormant.
There is a cycle, never still.
For both, the seasons move
and there comes to each a spring.

Love: a Meditation

"Love" says Webster, "is a feeling of strong personal attachment." And so it is, but that hardly says the half of it, for there are so many kinds of love.

There is the strong, natural, outpouring love of a child for his mother and father and their warm, protecting love for him. This love may be almost taken for granted, but it is there—a tough rope as enduring as life itself.

There is the love of a young man for a maid and her love for him—sunny golden threads that finally weave themselves into church bells, a bridal veil, and the establishment of a new home.

There is the love of either man or woman for the chosen life career. It may be homemaking, or business, or art. Whatever it is, it too calls for the response which is known as "love"—this time a leather thong of attachment.

Yes, love is all of these and more. It is standing alone at night under a star-studded sky and feeling a sudden awareness of kinship with the whole wide world. It is looking deep into the heart of a perfect rose and seeing in that beauty the perfection of God's planned universe.

And love is a golden chain, linking each soul to God. This love is a gift from God, poured out freely. As we become aware of it, we grow as does the seed when warm sun urges it to fulfillment. As we pour out that love into the world, more and more of it flows through us. This love can heal a sick body, bring abundance, harmonize. This love is made up of all lesser loves, fused into our love for God and His love for us—this love is the essence of life, this love is the reason for life!

Silence

Dear Father, teach me silence.
I would learn to find within
That place of quietude, of peace,
Wherein You often speak to me
In an hour of prayer and praise;
But I would learn to find it
In that crowded pause in time
Wherein an elevator descends,
In the paragraph between two stops
Of a subway's hurtling passage,
In the noisy vocal static
Of the lunch counter where I eat.
This is a world of high decibels;
I would learn to balance them
With a frequent inner turning
To a Truth of peace, of stillness.
So, Father, will I learn to find You
Throughout the busy hours of living.
Dear Father, teach me silence.

Time Enough

I take time for prayer, and I have time left for all else! This I have proven for myself; so may you prove it, if you will.

If we take time first of all for prayer, then time is left for all else we must do. This is true because prayer so orients us that we begin to function in God and in Him only.

Let us start our day with prayer. Let us enter into the silent place within our own being and wait for the presence of God to be revealed to us. Let us pray with words and without words. Let us listen, listen to hear what God would say to us.

With our praying, with our listening, comes a plan for the day. There comes an intuition, perhaps, of some change we should make. Or perhaps we only know that step by step our way will be ordered through every moment and every hour.

As we take time for prayer we find that there is time left for all else we need to do; and there is the wisdom, the strength, and the power to do it.

Not Your Day?

Did you ever say, "Oh, this is just not my day!" as a sort of excuse when you missed your regular bus, got to the office and found you'd left some important papers at home—when things were just generally out of sorts?

Well, you were right, the day wasn't yours—but it was God's. No day belongs exclusively to us; all days belong to God. And the one sure way to straighten out the kinks when you feel the day is "just not your day" is to begin to realize that the day is God's day. It is when we forget this that things go wrong.

This is not my day; this is God's day. A day begun with this affirmation will never turn into the kind of comedy of errors that afflicts most of us once in a while. And if a day begins to come apart at the seams, it can be realigned immediately with that same affirmation.

This in not my day; this is God's day. The emphasis is where it belongs—on God. Instead of being all-important, I become a channel through which God may work. When I recognize God's importance in my life, and that my importance comes only in letting the life of God flow through me into the world, then tangled affairs straighten out, accomplishments are made, and I am serene—at peace with God, at peace with myself, and at peace with my world.

Words

The Truth
is not
to heal the body,
to fill the purse,
to harmonize the situation,
to perfect all.

The Truth
is
the body healed,
the purse filled,
the situation harmonized,
all perfected—
now.

Lenten Devotion

Dear God, illumine now my mind!
Show me how to gain
within this Lenten season
a new spiritual depth,
increased inner vision,
a growing awareness of Thee.

Dear God, illumine now my mind!
Show me how to deny, erase,
whatever is not of Thee
in every area of my life,
cleansing my whole being.

Dear God, illumine now my mind!
I would let Thy radiance
shine unclouded into my mind,
into my soul, into my body,
that I may become, indeed,
transfigured for Thee.

Dear God, illumine now my mind,
that I may show forth
in the unfolding pattern of days,
a reflection of Thee alone.
This, my Lenten prayer.

A CELEBRATION OF MARCH

Contemplation

No longer tethered
by the string of mind,
the heart,
lifted by love,
is a balloon
soaring up, up, up
into the blue sky
of Spirit.

Colors are brighter,
sounds clearer,
touch more sensitive,
mind more perceptive
after prayer.

Deep meditation
reaching into the heart
of the inner silences
turns what a man is
inside out.

Spiritual Transformers

Electrical workers know that voltage can be increased or decreased by the use of transformers. These transformers have their counterpart in the world of spiritual reality.

The flow of spiritual energy in a life is constantly passing through one or another of the transformers. This happens whether one is aware of it or not. Spiritual energy is either being increased or decreased; and as one learns to understand the nature of spiritual energy, he can control its transformation.

A positive consciousness is a "step-up" transformer. As the unceasing flow of energy enters this consciousness, its power is increased, and it manifests in outer works as directed by the mind. However, a negative consciousness acts as a "step-down" transformer that weakens and devitalizes the flow of energy so that little or none is available to manifest outwardly.

Every man has within himself the ability to develop the kind of transformer he wants to use. A look at his life will tell him whether the energy, the life force, is being stepped up or stepped down. If he finds his consciousness acting as a "step-down" transformer, it is possible for him to contact the "master maintenance shop" and have it remade to increase the voltage. This contact is made through prayer, daily prayer, in which he lays his problem before God and asks for guidance and for renewal.

As this process is going on, he must keep a close watch on his thoughts, attitudes, words, and actions. He must try to keep them oriented to the positive consciousness he is developing. He must not unwittingly undo the changes made during prayer by his actions the rest of the day. Affirmations will help maintain the right feeling; they will, in fact, act as small but effective "step-up" transformers in themselves.

When one learns to keep the spiritual energy passing constantly through transformers which increase, not decrease, its power, one finds his whole life being revitalized. His perception and understanding are quickened; abilities develop swiftly; human relationships become more rewarding. He becomes, in fact, a "stepped-up" person.

Infusion

I AM God's creation.
I AM filled with His life.
I AM illumined by His light.
I AM strengthened by His power.
I AM infilled with His love.
I AM imbued with His wisdom.
I AM released into His will.
I AM lifted up to His transformation.
I AM alive eternally in Him.
I AM God's creation.

God Bless You Now

My day is full of blessings that I give away. Just the silent words, "God bless you now," and a tiny thread of thought links your heart to God in closer union for a moment in the space of time. What lift you get, what sudden easing of the load you bear, I never know. I only know my own day is more joyous and my way more sure.

I need not know your name: you sell me bread or leave a letter in my box—I send a blessing with you on your way. I need not see your face: your newsboy's whistle in the dusk will bring a quick response, "God bless you now." Perhaps your name comes to my mind in a sudden swift awareness for no reason I can give: "God bless you now, and keep you in His name."

You who live with me in this same house, could you but see the words my mind and heart are forming you would know I say "God bless you" all the day.

Yes, I bless you, all of you, dear friends and strangers both, and yet my blessing books can never balance—I receive in such great measure blessings all the while.

A Housewife's Meditation

Dear Father-God, bless me as I go about my daily household tasks. Give me of Your untiring strength; help me to organize every job so that it may be done quickly and well.

As I cook and clean, as I answer the telephone, as I shop and plan, let me feel Your presence close beside me. You are my strength and patience. You are my wisdom and inspiration. Let me serve You as I serve the ones I love.

Bless the food that I prepare. Let it fill the needs of each body; let it give strength and energy; let it give life and health.

Bless the family gathered at the table. Let each mealtime be a happy time, a time of communion and companionship. And when the meal is done, dear Father, be with each member of the family as he goes his way.

Dear Father, bless this house, bless this family, bless us all this day. Fill us with Your peace; warm us with Your love; lift us with Your joy.

This my prayer, my faith, today.

Thought - Starters

Is there one time of day when you always feel closest to God?

How would you devise a spiritual achievement test?

Are you living in the kingdom of God right now—today?

Do you ever need brakes in a spiritual experience?

Did you make a gift to anyone today—a tithe not necessarily of money but of time or talents or gifts of the Spirit?

Some Thoughts about Silence

Our universe has become a noisy one! In the city, sirens scream; taxis blow their strident horns; whistles, blowtorches, even conversation is noisy. In the country, jet planes rocket past overhead; tractors chug; heavy transport trucks rumble by on the highways. In our homes, radio and television sets assault our ears; telephones ring; doorbells buzz.

Yet we know that growth occurs in silence. In the quiet of sleep the body grows, is renewed, rebuilt. In the silence of deep thought the mind grows; in the silence of prayer, communion with God, the soul grows.

Perhaps with less noise, with more silence, our growth would be more pronounced. So I would schedule my day to include as much silence as possible. I turn the radio or television on only to get a special program. I pick a regular time for quiet prayer, and muffle the telephone for that hour.

As I think about silence, I begin to appreciate more fully some of the silent things: the deep star-studded silence of a summer night or the thick silence of a new-fallen snow; the unspoken love of a friend expressed in a smile, a handclasp, an act of service; the silent perfection of a single rose; the silence of printed words in a matchless line of prose or poetry.

If the pattern of my life is essentially a noisy one, I seek now for ways to cultivate the joy of a silent hour each day. If I already have quiet times, I give thanks and enter into them completely. In the silences some of the sweetest harmonies of life are played.

Spring

I read the signs:
    the swelling leaf buds
    on a winter-bare tree,
    an early robin pecking
    at frozen apples;
I listen for the cues:
    the creaking of an ice jam
    on the waterway,
    the wild free honking
    of the first northing geese;
I feel a rising in my own heart
    as the orbit of the earth
    turns toward the spring,
    a faith in the ordering
    of God's universe.
I give thanks for spring.

Creation

I bless this idea,
A seed planted in my mind and soul
By the same creative Spirit of God that made the
earth.

I nurture this idea—
Feed it thoughts of love and wisdom—
Water it with faith and strength and joy and life.

I develop this idea
Through constant prayer and praise
Until it is embodied in a concrete plan of action.

I act on this idea-plan,
Guided by the very Presence of the hand of God,
And slowly, but so surely, bring it to its full fruition.

This plan-idea is now become a fact,
Seen and heard and felt by men—manifest.
So does God's perfect kingdom come on earth, and
only so.

Spiritual Immunization

Divine love is my spiritual immunization against all negation. This love surrounds me. It is within and without. It is part of my blood and bone and brain. It is manifest in the people about me, in the wind and air and sun. It is God's great gift, His healing life pouring out upon me. I rest in that love; I let it have its divine way with my soul, with my body, with my affairs, with my whole life. It comforts and heals; it blesses and inspires me; it frees me from every bondage, from every fear.

With God's love surrounding me, no negative thought can gain a hold in my mind, no negative word can pass my lips, no negative action can be carried out. But not only within me—neither can any negation from outside touch my life in any way. No outer power can make me sick, harm me in any way, bring me any kind of ill fortune. I am truly immunized against negation and all its ill effects.

Divine love, God's love, makes me safe from every form of negation, be it a suggestion of personal doubt, a fear of some outer influence, or some apparent disaster. Love casts out every fear! With love my constant immunization, I meet every challenge of my life victoriously.

Rise To New Life

Now does the very earth prepare for life! The days lengthen; sap rises in the maple; there is a stirring in the root, the stem, the bud.

I also prepare now for the festival of life, for the day of resurrection. I look deep within to the hidden roots of my being. I search out my deepest beliefs, the hidden causes of my actions.

I pray for a cleansing of fear, of apathy. I pray for the dissolution of the doubts and negations that have slowly built barriers between my soul and God. I seek a wiping away of all separation.

I meditate on the changing seasons of earth, the changing seasons of man. A time of preparation is a time of change. It is a time to deny the imperfect and make ready to accept the perfect.

As I pray and meditate, daily, I feel an upsurge of expectancy. The season rises toward the Spring equinox and as it rises, so does my heart rise toward Easter. I await the Eastertide with great eagerness.

On Good Friday, I symbolically extinguish the hearth fire in my heart, the fire that will be rekindled with the glowing Christ Light on Easter morning. This early Christian custom reminds me that Christ is indeed the Light of the world. I make ready to receive that Light with love, with praise, with adoration—my heart cleansed and purified through prayer.

Dear God, now do I cleanse my being and prepare for new life.

The Robe of Christ

Seamless it was,
luminous,
finely woven and without
blemish;
to touch but the hem
brought healing.
As He hung upon the Cross,
soldiers cast lots
and one
carried it away.
Where?
Is there a single fiber
left today,
or has it crumbled
into dust,
the dust of the earth?
I walk a dusty road . . .
is there some essence
of that shining robe
here?
I feel Christ
very near . . .

Credo for Easter

I believe
In the risen Christ,
In the stone rolled back,
In the angel's voice:
"Why seek ye the living among the dead?
He is risen!"

I believe
In the sprouting seed,
In the springtime blossoming,
In the greening field.

I believe
In the eternal resurrection
Of hope, of love, of joy,
In the fresh upspringing of faith,
In the wonder of answered prayer.

I believe
In Christ risen from the dead
In everlasting victory
Of life!

Arise! Arise!

Arise, this is the time of resurrection! As Jesus arose living and triumphant from the grave, arise all of you who are in bondage to illness or lack of any kind. Arise triumphant as He did. Jesus said, "He who believes on me will also do the works that I do; and greater works than these will he do." Arise, sleep no more!

Speak the word of faith to every cell in your body. There is divine intelligence in every cell. Call upon this intelligence to arise to perfect form, perfect function, perfect health. This is the time of resurrection; call to the sleeping cells. Command them to awaken to new life.

Speak the word of faith to every situation in which lack seems to manifest itself. With God all things are possible. Rejoice! Rejoice! This is the time of rejoicing; this is the day you can awake to an awareness of God's limitless abundance of every good thing. Call it into your life now.

Arise, arise, arise! Let the light of God's love shine upon you. Let the radiance of His Spirit shine out through your very being. Arise! Arise!

A CELEBRATION OF APRIL

Prescription for Prayer

Prepare a silent place—
    for this a stillness in the mind
    is vital
    and is helped by a private
    and a quiet room;
Add a yearning heart
    that longs to know God
    with a deep, unspeakable desire;
Let there be a waiting time,
    live and expectant
    (passivity will always fail);
Soon there will come
    a radiance, a glow,
    an electric kind of knowing
    the presence of God
    deep within.
This is prayer.

Spring Sunshine

All sorts of things
Bloom in the spring sun.
Not only the crocus,
Not only violet and redbud;
Puppies burst into a frill
Of running in circles
And tumbling over each other;
A bluebird's song
Is petaled in pure joy;
And an old, old lady
On a park bench,
Well bundled up against chill wind,
Is as truly flowering
As any fragile hyacinth.

Soul Conditioners

Just as the garden soil needs conditioners to keep it in a productive state, so does the soul need conditioners if it is to produce an abundant spiritual harvest. Here are some effective soul conditioners whose use may increase soul growth and widen spiritual horizons.

Prayer, faithful daily prayer, is a necessity for spiritual growth. Pray for others as well as for yourself; pray for world leaders; pray for peace.

Worship with others adds depth to soul growth. Join with others regularly in church on Sunday; start a prayer group that meets regularly; make family worship a meaningful adjunct to living.

Bless all who come in contact with you; bless everything you use during the day; bless every condition and circumstance of your life. This can condition your life so that its own productivity is trebled.

Tithe to condition your soul as well as your affairs. Tithe time and talent, material things and intangibles, as well as money.

Cleanse negation from your mind and heart and soul to give spiritual growth a chance to flower. Use denials, a quick on-the-spot mental eraser to release each and every negative thought and attitude as soon as it enters your mind.

Memorize affirmations, meaningful poetry, Bible verses to increase your spiritual conditioning. Make words of power yours to call upon in time of stress, during a sleepless hour when a problem so fills your mind that you cannot instantly release it to God.

Walk with God daily, hourly, momently. Make the practice of the presence of God a constant habit.

How wonderfully you will be blessed!

Take these soul conditioners and make them your own. Then do your own research to find new, effective formulas for spiritual vitamins, for soul conditioners that will help you and others, as you share your findings, to experience an ever deepening, widening, more fruitful spiritual growth.

A Mini - Prayer

Dear God,
Give me the light
To see the shadow
For the nothingness it is.

         Amen.

Healing Hands

Dear Father-God, here are my hands. Take them; use them! Show me where You need them. Fill them with Your power and love and compassion.

As I touch a feverish child, a cripple, or any other with great need, I put my own consciousness of self aside. These hands are Your hands. Use them for bringing the pattern of Your perfection, Your health and beauty into manifestation. They are but an instrument for Your use. Through them flows Your great love which can heal any disease, any apparent evil whatsoever. With You are all things possible. Use my hands as You will, to bring the Truth, the reality, into visible form in man, woman, or child.

Of myself I can do nothing; it is You, Father, sending Your love and strength and power through me; it is You alone who can bring healing.

Dear Father, I give You my hands. Take them; use them, to heal the sick and wipe away suffering. Use them however You will. Take them and use them, now and forever.

Amen.

Joy

Joy springs up in my heart today! This is a glad, new day. Spring is upon the land; the air feels soft and lifegiving. Green things are shooting up all about, even in the cracks in city pavements. New life is everywhere appearing.

In my heart, too, there is new life, a reawakening of joy, happiness, light, and love. How wonderful to be alive! The world rejoices, and I rejoice that life is everlasting, that it ever springs forth anew.

Joy, joy, joy! The words sing in my heart as I do my work. They bring me new inspiration, new zest with which to accomplish my usual tasks. They bring me a joyous peace. All will finally be right with the world. My own problems, which loomed so large on dark winter days, now appear in proper perspective. I see that they are opportunities for me to prove God's laws. So, with joy, I meet them. And this great wellspring of joy so breaks down old barriers of pride, resentment, fear, and doubt that God's perfect solutions become immediately apparent and instantly manifest.

Joy, joy, joy! These words sing in my heart all the day long!

A Prayer for Guidance

Dear God, in Your hands
I place myself on this day.
Your purpose for my life,
Your perfection for my body,
Your abundance for my need—
In Your hands lie these,
And their fulfillment in my life
Is sure if by my will and my desire
I too am totally in Your hands.
Guide me, then, in Your ways
Throughout the whole of this day—
Free my mind of fear and doubt
That I may think creatively,
Free my body of its limitations
That it may be strong and vital,
Free my spoken word of hesitation
And my action from indecision.
In Your hands I place my total self
For I am Yours, dear Father-God.

Prayer at Midnight

Dear Father-God: All is dark—the only light a lesser darkness and a grayer shadow. Small night noises are but exclamation points to silence. And I alone am awake.

Now are You very near to me; or is it not that I, in the stillness, have reached nearer unto You? For now the soul is free to wander—out, in the farthest spaces and in, to the depths of being ever-unperceived in light of day. I, alone, awake and commune with You.

Filled with the wonder of Your presence, I ask Your blessing on those I love. As I say their names I see Your presence around each one—healing the pain, filling the lack, supplying the answer to what-ever the need may be. It matters not how many miles of earth and sky and sea may lie between; now are they, all unknowing, drawn closer to You. And my heart again can rest.

Still, still is the dark, but radiant my soul shines out with light. Yours is the presence, the time, the space, the all. And I have been a part of this immen-sity. I, alone, awake.

Amen.

Spring Carol

Sing crocus and snowdrop,
a green leaf, a grass-blade;
sing redbud and wild plum
and crab apple bloom;
sing of the snow melting
and the dark earth stirring
in a warming sun, to robin's call.
Sing all these—
Sing Spring!

Credo for Accomplishment

I will begin each new day with prayer, feeling with my inner spirit for oneness with God, stating my purposes for the day, listening for guidance.

I will begin each new task, whatever it may be, with a turning toward God, renewing of assurance that He is with me.

I will let go of the tenseness of hurry and frustration. (A delay may be the saving hand of God holding me back from danger or preparing the way for my greatest good.)

I will recognize in all material things the expression of God's limitless supply; I will use freely and wisely that which I have, knowing that every need will be met on time.

I will recognize the Christ Spirit in every worker; I will praise, not criticize; I will give a helping hand without any feeling of irritation.

I will let God's love and joy and compassion flow out through me to all those whose lives touch mine.

I will see in all my affairs the wondrous pattern of God's plan working out piece by piece, making use of my ever-growing capacity for accomplishment, giving a needed service to other lives, and bringing to my heart and soul the knowledge of fulfillment.

Spiritual Sunlight

Now do I go apart from the world. I close the outer door that I may not be distracted by people. I sit comfortably relaxed, still and serene.

Now I close the door of my mind on the outer things. Peace, peace, I say. I rest now, quietly, without word, without thought, without emotion. Peace, be still.

Now I center my attention, my concern, on God the Father. I look to Him, peacefully relaxed, serene and quiet.

Slowly I begin to feel that inner stillness grow and encircle me. A sort of spiritual sunlight envelops me. I am warm and comforted. I am quiet with a living quietness. Here, in this holy communion with my Father-God, I am re-created. I am healed. I am blessed in all ways. And I am shown the way that He would have me go, the work that He would have me do.

I am enveloped in the spiritual sunshine of divine love—both loving and receiving love within that radiant glow. And I give thanks.

Amen.

Thought-Starters

If you are an employer, do you think your employees ever consider you a "problem boss"? If you are an employee, does your supervisor ever consider you, or have reason to consider you, a "problem worker"?

What connection is there between thought pollution and air pollution?

Did you ever use prayer to get a parking place?

Is there a spiritual "generation gap"?

Do you consider time spent in prayer preparation, in "centering down" as the Quakers put it, as important as time spent in actual prayer?

Prayer for Travelers

Now do the hours, the miles, pass by—
Dear Lord, be with each one who goes
To some different place beyond the sky
Or simply down a narrow road he knows.
The traveler needs You by his side
As he journeys to whatever place,
And do we not all take life's ride
Upon a planet traveling in space?
Dear Lord, be with us on our way—
We travel, all of us, each day.

Growth

The seed,
then the roots
downward,
and the stem shoots
upward
toward the light;
so my life
also
has the outer,
the visible part
counterbalanced
by the deeper,
inner
growth.

Prayer for Growing Things

Dear God, bless all the growing things there are in earth, in sky, in ocean depth. Bring fulfillment from the dream; the harvest bountiful from tiny seed. Bless the growingness in life.

Bless plants, dear God, that they may grow from sprouting seed to springing stalk and ripe harvest. Let each plant fill the need in Your plan. Bless scurrying insects, busy in their way, growing from egg to larva, pupa and adulthood. Bless the growth of animal and bird, snake and fish, and of every form of life.

And oh, dear God, bless the growth of man throughout the whole life span, from childhood to youth to maturity. Bless the growth of each physical body that it may show forth that perfection innate within its being. Bless each mind that it may ever reach out to new horizons, seeking new wisdom, encompassing more and more of Your plan. And, most especially, bless that soul growth which is distinct in man . . . growth in which he reaches both within and without himself to You, yearning to know You, eager to fulfill his own spiritual destiny, pushing toward a spiritual maturity that knows no boundary in years.

Dear God, bless all of life and all of growing, that it may be fulfillment in Your sight.

Amen.

A New Prayer

Dear God,
make me new;
newly eager
to find You
in man,
in the universe;
newly responsive
to You
in relationships,
in situations;
newly pledged
to pray,
to be guided,
and to be,
each new day,
a new channel
for You
in my world.
Amen.

A CELEBRATION OF MAY

God Goes with Me

God goes with me when I walk at dawn. His hand points out the beauty of my path, shows sunrise shadows or the rhythm of a bird's first morning flight. He leads me in peace and loveliness wherever I walk.

God goes with me when I go at noon through crowded ways. His is the power that speeds me safely on my way. And when I mingle with the crowd it is His inspiration that gives me confidence.

If my way lies over water, it is God's rhythm that I hear in throbbing engines, see in unfurled sail. His is the voice that speaks to wind and wave, His the pole to which the navigator's compass turns, His the star by which is reckoned time and space.

God goes with me if I go by air. I see below the green-field patterns and the city blocks. His is the world and all that is within, above, below. I am His and He is mine.

It makes no difference how I go—by land or sea or air—God goes with me all the way.

Let Go

Let go, today, of all that worries you.
Alone, in silence, loose your doubt and fear.
"Come unto me . . . and I will give you rest."
In prayer, let go all tension and draw near
To Him who seeks, right now, right here, to bear
Your burden, free you from it, and release
You from all limitation. Can you dare
To take this step, go forward filled with faith,
All worries gone, forgotten, cast away?
Of course! You are a living son of God;
You feel His presence with you when you pray;
You know His peace, His wisdom, and His love;
His strength is yours to call upon, to use;
His joy within you is a radiant light
That blesses others as it blesses you.
Let go! Stand forth, perfected in His sight.

Spiritual Housecleaning

Time for spring housecleaning? Then perhaps it's time for spiritual housecleaning too. Mind and soul need a general cleaning to remove unnecessary clutter and wipe away the dust of negation that tarnishes the richness of life. Beliefs and ideas need sorting and straightening. The soul must be made clean and shining; then it will be ready to receive new spiritual possessions.

Four steps will accomplish spiritual housecleaning: denial, forgiveness, affirmation, and consciousness of at-one-ment.

Denial gets rid of unwanted ideas and beliefs—fear, envy, pride, intolerance. Search deep for your own spiritual "fire hazards" and throw them out. Through the power of God in you, deny their hold on you. Get rid of them.

Use the vacuum cleaner of forgiveness next. Forgive yourself for shortcomings, forgive others for real or fancied slights and hurts. Make this a real cleansing of the soul, getting rid of every speck of negative dust. How brightly the light of spirit can shine when this is done!

Now, with strong affirmations of Truth, fill the spiritual spaces you have cleaned. Affirm your spiritual beliefs. Place your true desires here, surrounded by faith, love, joy.

When this is done, rest in conscious at-one-ment with God. Pray that His Presence be with you and stay with you. Love will come, joy will come, and peace will be yours. You will know divine order.

Step forth now, confident and unafraid into the world, but daily return in prayer to the shining inner sanctuary of your soul.

Morning Rhythm

I go to meet my good!
Head high, back straight and tall,
A quick firm stride to match
A silent bugle call
That musters gathering faith,
New-fed on morning prayer.
Alive with joy and praise,
My heart and soul declare:
In all I do, in every way,
I go to meet my good today!

Born Anew

I am born anew and I see as God sees!

I am born anew through the knowledge of the power of the Holy Spirit indwelling. I put aside the old self, the self that sees good and evil, the self that acknowledges lack, the self that fears disease. As the water cleanses that over which it flows, as the wind blows away the dust, so these beliefs are washed away and dispersed by the power of the Holy Spirit.

I am born anew as I accept the idea that the Holy Spirit, the Spirit of God, is working in and through and for me in every possible way. I am lifted up by the power of the Holy Spirit. Clear and creative thinking are mine, and a good memory is mine. Health that radiates through every cell, muscle, bone, organ, and function is mine. Prosperity in running-over measure is mine. Harmony that unifies and blesses all my relationships is mine. Peace that fills my heart, home, and world is mine.

Through knowing the power and the presence of the Holy Spirit, I am born anew and I "see the kingdom of God."

Credo for Every Day

I am
A perfect child of God,
Created in His image
And after His likeness.

I am
Perfect health,
Each cell filled with life,
Functioning in perfect order.

I am
Love and wisdom,
Strength and harmony,
Peace and joy and creative power.

I am
Prosperity,
Receiving abundantly of all good,
Pouring abundance out into the world.

I am
His heir,
In all things, in all ways,
A perfect child of God.

God's Abundance Is Mine

Divine substance, from which everything visible and invisible is made, knows no limitation. Lack is manmade. Abundance is God's—and abundance is man's in whatever measure he accepts it.

I accept God's abundance now. I am filled with the knowledge, the realization, the understanding that there is plenty of every good thing. The unlimited substance of God is mine to call upon and use. My mind is alert to His creative ideas. I have the understanding to put these ideas into action. As I put these creative ideas into action, spiritual substance takes perfect form and I have an abundant supply to meet every need.

I do not limit the number of ideas I receive, nor do I limit the avenues of expression whereby I put these ideas into action. I trust God for ideas to meet small needs as well as large needs. I accept God's abundance in bountiful measure and every need is met.

God's abundance is mine, and I accept His abundance now!

In Silence

The moon
sends ripples of light
into the darkness
of the pond,
the shadows
dappled
by drifting clouds;
so does faith
send its shaft
of hope and peace
into consciousness
as I drift
into the darkness
of sleep.

Thought - Starters

Could you pray effectively through the medium of drawing, making music, or dancing?

Do you have spiritual curiosity?

When a problem comes up, do you look for the "growth opportunity" it is hiding?

Do you ever shut the door on that inner nudging which is God's guidance?

Do you have a spiritual stockpile? How big is it?

Peace

Sing peace
from a quiet heart.
Let peace flow
out   out   out
to the everywhere,
to the nowhere,
into timelessness.
Let peace spark
into new forms
of communion,
into new questions,
into new answers.
Let peace build
upon itself
even where there is
no peace at all,
until peace
finds itself there.
Sing peace
from a quiet heart.

Prayer Sentences for Protection

The very light of God surrounds me now with an impenetrable force field of protection.

I walk in safety for I walk with God.

The very light of God dissolves every fear thought arising in my mind and every thought of evil proceeding toward me from any other mind.

The armor of God is woven of prayer, faith, use—but in itself it is a gift of God.

God-with-me-now—I need no other protection.

A Miracle, to God

A miracle, to God, is a natural happening. What joy sings in my heart as I realize that nothing . . . truly, nothing at all . . . is impossible to God! A miracle, to Him, is perfectly natural. It is brought about by spiritual laws operating through material means in ways that we do not as yet understand.

Does this surprise you? Does pushing a button and seeing a light bulb glow strike you as a miracle? Does it seem miraculous to get into an airplane and fly? Or watch on a TV set as astronauts journey beyond this planet into space? To me, yes, these all seem a little like miracles, yet I find myself taking them rather for granted in a way no one alive a hundred years ago could have. Such a man would surely have called radio, TV, frozen foods, a helicopter all miracles—to say nothing of an orbiting spaceman!

So, surely, will other wonderful things be developed. But even before they become commonplace, there are times when prayer plus faith bring today-miracles into being. There are "miracles" of health, of strength, of protection. There are miracles of tangled relationships straightened, of disaster averted, of "impossible" success. To God, these are "natural" happenings.

I remember often the words from Matthew, "With men this is impossible, but with God all things are possible." That's the way it is with miracles.

In Our Time

There is a rock
that stands
where it has always
stood.
There is a Man
who stands
where He has always
stood.
There is a song,
its vibrations ringing
galaxy-wide.
Listen!
There is a song
even
in our time.

Dream Your Dream

Look to the far horizons and spread your vision wide! Take the dream of your heart and live it out, for God is with you. The whole wide world is yours, for He has given you dominion, if you accept your place as His son.

Stifle not your dream of dreams! It was put in your heart by God. Think of Columbus who sailed the chartless seas to find a new world; of the men who built wings and took to the air when everyone said, "Impossible." Think of Helen Keller, in a dark and silent world, who yet lived a full and beautiful life. Think of these and, oh, so many more. Would you, then, let a handicap, an adverse opinion, a failure or two stop you? Oh, dream your dream and make it come true!

The world of Spirit, the world of mind, the world that is seen—these three worlds and all that is within them—let your spiritual vision encompass them and make them one. Expand your life and use the abilities God has given to you alone. Oh, dream your dream and live it out! Be not bound—but step out, free, with God!

Meditation on Death

I hold gently on my hand a little bird that has fallen to the ground. For a moment it rests, then it flies again and I see it no more. For a moment of God's time I clasp a hand in friendship and travel the path of life in companionship and love and joy. Then that one slips through the door that we call death and I see him no more. But I would no more grieve than for the bird that has flown. Loneliness, yes, and sorrow that the door between us is closed; sadness if there was pain in the passing. But I find joy in the realization that a new life, fresh strength, greater spiritual understanding, and further opportunity for the soul's triumph await.

Yes, I would save my grief for the soul who rejects God. I would fill my loneliness in seeking out and comforting the needy and the restless and the sick. I would spend my sorrow on the stuff of spiritual joy—closer companionship with God, deeper insight into His love, and a greater understanding of prayer. I would not fear death, for myself nor for another, knowing it to be only a step into a higher realm, knowing that one day there will be no death.

No Limits

Imagination
opens up new worlds,
dissolves apathy,
closes the time gap
between inception
of a dream
and its reality.

Affirmation
focuses the lens
of prayer
to bring to view
the true vision
of what is.

Manifestation
mirrors
in an outer form
the inner creation
in realization
of truth.

A CELEBRATION OF JUNE

"And God Saw that It Was Good"

There is the good earth,
and men have called it so
who have seen it from
the threshold of space;
there is the good moon,
and men have walked upon it
in its "magnificent desolation";
and there is a galaxy waiting,
and galaxy upon galaxy beyond . . .
there is no ending,
just as there is no limitation
to the double reach of man
thrusting out to the stars,
thrusting within to learn
the miracle of his own being.
The whole of *creation*
is not yet imagined . . .

Morning Meditation

A skyline streak of crimson heralds the dawn and a lingering star fades slowly. A breath of breeze pays an early morning call, and birds begin to twitter sleepily. This is a new day.

Before material thoughts intrude I lead my conscious mind to that still haven of my soul where my own indwelling Christ opens wide the doorway of my heart. At once, mind, soul, and body, I am flooded with the light and love of God my Father. I am lifted high above the earthly plane and filled with the radiance of Spirit.

Almost without conscious thought I send this love and light on to those whom I hold most dear, that it may lift them, heal and comfort them. As I send this radiance on I am filled anew with power, and I release this power to the whole world to lift and guide and bless.

The sun's rays call me and a day's tasks await me. But God is very close, and with His help all shall be done perfectly.

Evening Meditation

Darkness is creeping over the silent hills, and a little new moon is tossing handfuls of twinkling stars across the heavens. Bird whisperings are the only sounds. As stillness settles down upon me I look back upon the day.

Beauty was here today to lift my heart. Love was here to lift my soul. Joy led me swiftly on my way, and Christ in me pointed out the path when I was suddenly confused.

This was a good day, not perfect, but a day of some achievement, a day in which some inner fears were released, a day in which a new and greater love radiated from God through me and from me to those I met.

Now silently I turn toward God and feel Him very close and dear. I offer this, my day, as my own gift, and ask His care throughout the night for myself and for those I love.

With His Spirit abiding in my heart I drift on clouds of sleep and, drifting, dream sweet dreams of peace.

Spiritual Climate Control

A thermostat called expectancy controls spiritual climate, and the thermostat can be turned up at will.

Spiritual climate may be described as the total environment of the soul, the individual spirit. Because man is a unified being—body, mind, and spirit—this climate is vital to every aspect of life. And he *can* exercise control over it.

The control mechanism is expectancy, the whole attitude of anticipation toward life. If we expect little from life, then we get little. If we expect trouble, disaster, difficulty, we should not be surprised when these come, as they surely will. But just as surely, we find all of our projects and all of the happenings in our life intermeshing in harmony and moving toward perfection when we expect only good.

If you feel dissatisfied with the picture somewhere, the spiritual climate needs improvement. The thermostat of expectancy needs to be turned up.

There are several ways to do this, but the hand of faith is the surest. As we meditate in faith, realizing that an abundance of all good has already been created for our use and is waiting for us to claim it, expectancy begins to rise. There comes a great infilling of joy, as we see life in a new light. The wonder of God's love shines within us. Gratitude wells up in our hearts.

Wherever the thermostat of expectancy is set now, it can be turned up. As the spiritual climate improves, all the blockages of doubt and fear are dissolved. In this Truth-filled climate, wonderful miraculous things happen in our life. The body is healed; the mind is quickened; abundance is manifest; the soul knows peace. And we are more truly, deeply alive than ever before!

Prayer Sentences for Peace

There is but one cosmic reality, God; the true balance of this reality is peace.

I maintain an inner balance and my world manifests peace.

There is one prayer to pray for the world: Peace . . . peace . . .

Peace: I pray peace; I think peace; I speak peace; I act peace; and, finally, I am peace—this my pleasure, my privilege, and above all, my obligation.

There comes an inner stillness, a point of rest; in that stillness, only peace!

Credo for Commencement

This I believe:

I am a child of God.

My perfect place awaits me.

I find it through steadfast prayer, backed by faith and implemented by action.

I am a brother to all men.

I prove the harmony of God in every situation by letting love and tolerance shine through every word and action.

I am heir with Christ.

An abundance of all good things is my birthright, which I now claim.

I am filled with the very light of life, surrounded by divine love, guarded by omnipotence, guided by omniscience.

Each day is a new gift.

I fill it with prayer and praise, with work and service, with relaxation and recreation—each in proper measure.

I continue to grow in Truth and spiritual understanding.

My own light shines.

I am a child of God.

Prayer for the Road

Ahead for many miles stretch out the wandering roads. Between the fertile fields of countryside, beneath tree-lined arches of small towns, along the crowded ways of cities go the roads. Dear God, ride by my side.

My way today may be long or short—ten minutes to school, three hours to a football game, or even clear across the country from north to south or east to west. Dear God, ride by my side.

Preserve me from sudden breakdown, from blowout, from any mechanical difficulty. Preserve me also from mental inattention, from daydreaming or carelessness or impulse to reckless show-off. Give me Your wise judgment as I drive, Your quick decision in emergency. Dear God, ride by my side.

But the road is not for me alone. Many another driver goes his way today; many a pedestrian is on the street; many a child is at play nearby. Stay the feet of the child who would dart into the road. Give the walker cautiousness and a watchful eye. And, dear God, ride with every other driver as well as by my side.

Make the road a shining way down which I travel safely on this day. Take me safely, quickly, surely to my destination. Please, dear God, ride by my side today.

Amen.

A Moment of Knowing

Up and up I had climbed
along a mountain path,
up beyond the tall spruce
to the high meadow land
where the fringed gentian
colored the field
as a blue depth filled
the bowl of sky above.
At the far edge of the meadow
a crystal spring bubbled up.
Here I sat down to rest
and to drink of the pure water.
A dragonfly, translucent,
hovered for a long moment
by my hand, and a bird call
sounded in the distance.
As I rested, there came a moment,
indescribable,
a moment in which I was filled,
filled to overflowing
with the very Presence of God,
and it was my soul
which in that moment
was satisfied.

The Rhythm of God

My day goes smoothly, easily, joyously when I observe the natural rhythm of life. I start my day with meditation and prayer. I eat wisely, not too much. I exercise moderately. I arrange my work so that I do not concentrate on one type of activity for more than two hours. I sleep as many hours as I need.

Today I do what lies before me to be done, without overconcern for the future, doing it as well as I can, easily and rhythmically. I release all tensions over past mistakes and misjudgments. Worries over health, over money, over family affairs, over employment—I give these to God, and accept in their place the assurance and security that is God's great gift.

As I relax the personal tensions that have held me rigid and straining, I am swept into the natural rhythm that pervades every particle of God's creation. The rhythm of the ebb and flow of the tides, of a bird's swift flight—these are mirrored in rhythmic timing of bodily function, and I experience increased bodily perfection. Every element of my life's activity shows new ease and joy as I move in time to God's rhythm.

My day goes smoothly, easily, joyously when I observe the natural rhythm of life, the rhythm of God.

Spiritual Identity

I cannot in any way express my identity without saying, "I am." And that *I AM* is indeed my true and spiritual identity. *I AM* is the indwelling Christ, the spiritual Self. It is the important, the identifiable part of me which manifests in the outer form. As the mind and body are one, so are soul and body one; but the outer form changes as it expresses more and more perfectly the one and constant *I AM*.

So today, very consciously, I would recognize my true identity. I am a son of God. I am filled with perfect health. I am endowed with creative abilities and I am now using those abilities to the glory of God on earth. I am receiving constantly my good, in overwhelming beauty and abundance. Oh, I am indeed a son of God; that is my true identity.

There is a tremendous power in the words "I am." I seek to discipline my thinking and my speaking so that I use these words only to identify myself with good, with my spiritual Self, my real Self. I use them daily to identify myself as a son of God, to identify myself with health of mind and body, with an abundance of all good, for this is my true identity—this is what and who *I AM*!

June

June is for joy;
    The earth's swift turning,
    A hot sun burning,
    Orioles' gay winging,
    A cardinal singing,
    Fragrant flowering,
    Quick-silver showering,
    Rainbow's fair ending,
    With all nature spending
    Joy in the greening—
    Joy in the June-ing.
June is for joy!

The Soul Takes Wings

"Talking about God is not the same as experiencing God. I have found that whenever prayer becomes an intimate feeling rather than an intellectual analysis, the soul consciousness takes wings," wrote Max H. Ballard.

And so, dear Father-God, I still the words of my heart. I rest in silence; I rest in You. As I rest I see anew with the inner eye the beauty of the universe; I see a radiance surrounding all that is of You. And as I see anew, so do I know and understand, more than ever before, something of the wonder of this universe and something of the magnificence of omnipresence and omnipotence.

Eternity—what is that but an everlasting "nowness," at one with You? An infinity? Is it not the "all-ness" of You? I am a part of both; I am a part of life; I am a part of You!

Now am I at peace, at home in the universe of Your creation. I feel You very near; I hear You in the silence; Your healing radiance envelops me. All is well. Amen.

"If I take the wings of the morning, and dwell in the uttermost parts of the sea, even there shall thy hand lead me, and thy right hand shall hold me."

Preparation for Prayer

Feet,
still, still now, upon the floor,
no need to hurry.

Hands,
lie quietly at rest,
no task to do just now.

Body,
relax in peace, serene;
now calmly rest.

Mind,
let go the scurrying,
let thought be still, so still.

Soul,
in silence vast as space,
reach, yearning, loving, unto God.

Replacing Fear with Faith

Through prayer I replace fear with faith.

The power of our faith makes all things possible. But when we fear, we block the channels through which the power flows. Thus we prevent the perfect outworking of good in our life.

Even though we know the effect of fear, we do not always take steps to conquer it. But there is a way to replace fear with faith. We do it through daily prayer, which enables us to feel a conscious oneness with God. Prayer by prayer, we develop the ability to keep our mind stayed on God, and fear thoughts arise less often. When such thoughts do come, we are alert to recognize them and we can immediately erase them with an affirmation of faith—faith in God and in our ability to do the thing we need to do.

We gain strength as we pray and then practice maintaining the feeling of God's presence with us, wherever we are, whatever we are doing. Through prayer we learn to live in faith, and we rejoice and give thanks for the good appearing in our life through the power of faith.

Through prayer I replace fear with faith—so must we remind ourself if fear creeps into consciousness.

Summer Storm

Dark, dark, roll in the clouds
ahead of a fury of wind
twisting the straining treetops,
flattening the green grass blades.
Oh, but there is glory in the storm!
I lift my face to the rain-lash:
    Cleanse me, God,
    of pride in self;
    strip me, God,
    of false pretence;
    wash from me, God,
    all prejudice;
    let me go free
    of all
    but Your concern.
Swiftly, swiftly, passes the storm.
The sun breaks through in a shower
of prism-sparkles against wet petals;
the brown thrasher in full voice again
and the swallowtail riding on air draft,
dust-free and greenly fragrant . . .
I, too, have been cleansed, made new.

A CELEBRATION OF JULY

Now

I pray
now,
at countless "nows"
each day.
I do it
now,
those little things
I'd rather do
some other "then."
I give thanks
now,
for little blessings,
each a small miracle
if I am aware.
I reach out
now,
to help another,
forgetting shyness.
I make
now,
rich with living.

Vacation Credo

I will take a vacation from hate,
From fear and worry, jealousy and envy;
I will take a vacation from greed,
False pride, intolerance, and prejudice.

I will journey to the still places
Where my soul can find its rest
In prayer, in meditation, in communion
With the Son, the Holy Spirit, and with God.

I will take a vacation from negation,
Will set my feet and mind in positive ways,
Will know with faith that with my God
All things whatsoever are possible to me.

Statement

What is fact
Speaks to my mind;
What is beauty
Feeds my soul;
What is challenge
Dares me to prove;
What is true
Makes me whole.

Timelessness

I walk with God in freedom from the limitations of time. There is within us something that rebels against the limiting and limited concepts of time. As Kahlil Gibran puts it, "the timeless in you is aware of life's timelessness." We need to enlarge the horizons of our view of time to encompass, insofar as we are able, eternity.

When we try to comprehend that which is without beginning or ending, with past, present, and future simply existing in the one Source, our concept of time will change. We will give up our "hurry philosophy," knowing that "with God all things are possible." This is as true of time as it is of healing or the filling of some great need.

The simple philosophy of walking with God each day, in a conscious close union with Him, will put our days on a more serenely ordered time pattern. We will find that we can more easily concentrate on the one job in hand, doing it to the best of our abilities with joy and efficiency. We will no longer waste time in idle daydreaming. What need is there for that, when all we could imagine and more comes to us when we put God first? Decisions will be quick and sure. And we will no longer feel the frustration of not enough time today for what must be done . . . or not enough time in a lifetime for all we desire to accomplish. There is *all time*. How greatly we need this truth!

Morning Commentary

To wake, dear God, to birdsong
is a joyous, lilting thing;
to wake to gentle falling rain
is an experience in peace;
to wake to patterned sunray
or to the silence of heavy snow,
or before the dawn when only
starshine dilutes the dark,
to wake, oh, it is to wake
that is the true gift, dear God.
I sing thanksgiving as I wake.

Thought-Starters

Does it take an emergency to enable you to "breakthrough" to God?

How much faith do you expend every day?

Does spiritual growth result in material gain?

Do you think an engineer will ever be able to measure the power of prayer?

If you could put in a long-distance telephone call to God, what could you think of to say to Him?

Summer Dreams

Oh, dear God,
please let all small children
dream of an open fire hydrant
and the silver splash
of cold water on their bodies.

Let old men dream dreams
of walking in green grass
in the early morning,
meeting the black and white cows
coming in to be milked.

Let the old women
rock to and fro in their sleep
to dreams of a porch swing
on a lazy flower-fragrant day.

So let each one dream
his separate, cooling dream
on this hot, still night,
and, oh, dear God,
let some of these dreams
come true!

Spiritual Evolution

Today I affirm: *"My whole consciousness is evolving into perfection."*

Spiritual evolution, the development of the consciousness into the perfection planned by God, is not tied to a time scheme. Each man and woman develops at his own pace, and can, by his thoughts and actions, slow or speed the process as he will.

Therefore I determine to work wholeheartedly toward this perfection, knowing that as I do so the tempo will quicken. I know that development of the spiritual faculties is dependent on my habitual attitudes of mind and spirit and so I resolve to erase the negative feelings and build positive habits. I know that being constant and regular in prayer and meditation fertilizes soul evolution. So does a practice of the presence of God throughout the day, no matter what I am doing or where I am, also pay big benefits, as I work to nurture soul growth.

Men and women help each other, too, in this spiritual ongoing. Prayer for others, an encouraging word, an example of strength under difficulty, a personal sacrifice to help another—these bless those about us, and we in turn are richly blessed. So, too, we must learn to accept freely spiritual help—prayers, suggestions, encouragement.

Spiritual evolution, the unfolding of the soul into its total perfection, is the basic business of life. I rejoice in my increasing awareness of this purpose, and in the process of spiritual evolution, now under way in my consciousness.

Credo for Summer

I believe
That this is God's season,
As indeed are all the seasons;
I delight in each day
And in whatever it brings
Of sun and rain, storm or calm.

I believe
That my safety lies with God,
As indeed it always does;
When I travel—by land, sea, or air—
I go safely, joyously, with Him.

O I believe
That to God belong all thanks,
For indeed He is Creator of all,
And so my thanks for summer's beauties,
For the season's change of pace,
Heightened hope, fresh creative thought,
A deepening understanding of life—
My thanks for all things go to God,
For I believe in God.

Prayer Sentences for Prosperity

There is only one life Force, only one life Substance, and only one life Supplier—God.

The one life Substance manifests in my life in every conceivable size, shape, form, in inconceivable abundance.

I give freely, without stint; I receive freely, without doubt.

Everywhere I look today there is an open door through which all good is walking to meet me.

I give thanks to God for the fulfillment of need when I first see/feel/think of the need—not after the need has been met.

There is truly one life Force, only one life Substance, and only one life Supplier, and through this One is abundance now manifest.

A Prayer for the World

Dear God, this is a wonderful world, this world in which we live. It is a world ever changing, ever growing, ever new. It is a world in which lie potentialities of abundance and freedom for every man, woman, and child. However, it is a world in which You have given us free will, to exercise salvation or to wreak terrible destruction as we choose.

Help us then, all the seeking, searching millions of us, to choose Your way, the way of life. Help our scientists to push, as they are fast doing, beyond the realm of the purely physical until they reach the spiritual realities of life underlying the whole universe and its pattern. Help every man and woman to take that step, to go beyond the things seen and felt and tasted and smelled, until they acknowledge from the heart and soul that You, our God and Father, are the source of life and the one way to life.

Help us, Father, those of us who are now acknowledging You, to be a leaven throughout every nation on every continent in every hemisphere to raise the whole body of the people into that same acknowledgment. Help us so to pray and so to work as to bring Your kingdom into earth as it is in heaven.

Dear Father, help every nation in the world to become a truly God-centered nation, acknowledging Your power, Your wisdom, Your mercy, and Your love. Let all leaders seek Your guidance. Let all the world choose the way, Your way, of life.

Amen.

Depth Perception

We see through prisms
variously colored,
through which shine
strangely distorted patterns
determining what we see,
and all the time
in our innocence
we believe we see
that which is outside.

Set Free

Today I am set free from every prison that has kept me from my perfect good.

From this day forth the prison doors of negation, fear, hatred, jealousy hold me back no more. I claim my sonship and go forth free. Divine love pours through me, renewing my confidence, dissolving old chains of bitterness, cleansing me of fear and indecision, and restoring my very life.

If I have been held back from my good, the prison walls have been of my own making, forged by deep-seated negative habits of thought and welded by petty selfishness. I see myself now freed from these habits, freed by at-one-ment with God and the laws of the universe. Through God I am now free, and I praise and give thanks that this is true.

My freedom and my resulting inner security are founded on the rock of God's omnipresence, omniscience, and omnipotence. I am free from every negative consciousness—disease, poverty, ugliness, inharmony. I am free from this day forward to eternity, with prayer the guardian of this freedom and spiritual growth the only requirement.

Today I am in Truth, and truly set free from every prison that has kept me from my perfect good!

Lesson in Relaxation

Peace. Peace. Be still.
Center down the weary mind.
Let the heart fill
With quietness, and find
Tensions departing
As stillness enters in
That center place and doubts
Slip off the rim
Of consciousness.
Fatigue will flee when Christ
Can come to bless,
For the soul enticed
To Him finds true release,
And rests, at peace.

As the Years Pass

I am eternally youthful in body, mind, and spirit! I rejoice that as the years pass I remain youthful— growing, learning, developing.

As I pray for health I am inwardly guided as to how best to care for my body so that it will remain vitally alive, functioning efficiently and painlessly throughout all the years of my life.

As I pray for mental guidance I am kept alert, receptive to new and better ideas. Instead of being rooted intellectually in the concepts and theories of the past, I look forward.

As I pray for spiritual development I am led to deeper insight into the Truth. By study, by inner searching, by prayer I grow constantly into a more truly spiritual person. In turn my spiritual growth shows in increased bodily perfection and intellectual achievement based on Truth.

No matter what may be my age in years, I greet each new day as a joyous adventure, for I am young in outlook and spirit. I am adaptable and I am growing constantly toward my Christ ideal, fashioning my life after the Christ pattern.

I rejoice that I am eternally youthful in body, mind, and spirit!

A CELEBRATION OF AUGUST

Psalms for the Summer

Sing praise!
Sing praise to God
for sun and sky and rain,
for grass and flower and fruit,
for sea and sand and sail-wind.
Sing praise!

Sing love!
Sing love to God,
love for the good earth,
love for all that lives,
love for plant and insect,
animal and bird and fish,
love for each man as brother.
Sing love!

Sing peace!
Sing praise of peace.
Sing love of peace.
Sing peace to earth, sky, sea.
Sing peace, sing peace
to all men—all men everywhere!
Sing peace
in love and praise of God!

Gifts of the Heart

"No man is so poor as to have nothing worth giving; as well might the mountain streamlets say they have nothing to give the sea because they are not rivers. Give what you have; to someone it may be better than you dare to think."—*Anon.*

What have I to give?
Oh, I am rich with gifts
Ready for the giving:
The gift of joy
That lights a shadowed spot;
The gift of perceptive praise;
The gift of thanks, its value
Doubled when unexpected.
There is the gift of faith
Wrapped in action, perhaps,
Or ribboned with words,
Or hidden deep within a prayer.
There is the gift of love,
A gift which, in the giving,
Is the gift of myself.
Oh, I am rich with gifts
And am constantly made richer
By the giving.

A Mini-Prayer

Dear God,
my talent
is a part
of Your pattern;
I use
my talent
in Your praise.
Amen.

A Vacation Prayer

God bless all vacationers.

God bless those who vacation at home. Let this vacation time be rich in meaning, let it be a time of rest and renewal, let it bring peace to mind and soul.

God bless those who sail in southern waters, climb snowcapped peaks, sun on sandy shores, or ride the western trails. Surround them with Your protecting presence, fill them with Your life and strength and joy.

God bless those who travel in strange lands. Let them see You in greeting smiles, let them hear Your voice in words of familiar accents or foreign tongue. Let their ways be made smooth and happy and free from worry or care.

God bless all vacationers. Open their eyes to the beauty all about them; open their minds to Truth everywhere; open their hearts to Your enfolding love.

Vision

Look up, to see a mountain peak!
Could any force except God's hand
Arrange in such majestic way
The contours of this rocky land?

Look out, to view an ocean's breadth!
No power could make immensity
Save God's own sure omnipotence
To call the waters into sea.

Oh look within, to depths of soul!
There shines, reflected, God's pure light.
Lit there upon creation's day . . .
And all found perfect, in God's sight.

God With Us

Wherever I go, I go safely, for God is with me.

In this age of swift travel when business, pleasure, or one of many other reasons sends us from place to place often, how comforting it is to know that God goes with us! It is a wonderful habit to precede every trip with a silent, inner knowing of the Truth—that God does indeed go with us to guide, to guard, to protect, to take us safely to our destination.

When a friend or loved one travels, how reassuring it is to know that we can affirm the Truth for him: that God goes with him wherever, however, whenever he goes. A friend always tells her traveling relatives and friends, "I'll pray you off!" This is a wonderful gift, the gift of prayer offered in a firm knowledge that God will indeed go with the traveler.

The inner security that comes from a knowledge of God's presence is a basic quality we all need in today's speeding world. The Psalmist sang of "The God who girded me with strength, and made my way safe." And so we pray: Dear Father-God, be with all travelers today. Let them feel the wonderful assurance of Your Presence. Amen.

Prayer Sentences for Health

There is only one life; that life circulates now through my body, cleansing, nourishing, healing, and perfecting.

I draw upon divine life to fill my body's lack.

The one life, manifested as healing light, radiates throughout my body so that I am aglow with health.

I give thanks today and every day for the exciting working of my body in perfection of mind-activity and soul-emotion interwoven with the functioning of blood, bone, organ.

The one life is my life; the one life is all life, forever.

I breathe now the breath of Spirit and I rejoice in life!

Prayer for the Atomic Age

Dear God, creator of our world
And other worlds flung far,
I see You in the atom's fusing
And in the evening star.

Your power is manifest in space
As well as in a seed,
Omniscient, omnipresent, yes,
Omnipotent to heed

The chaos of a world at birth,
A sailor's call at sea,
For You are all that is, that was,
That evermore will be.

Dear God, then fill my mind, my soul,
As Christ was filled, with You.
I would be filled with radiant life,
My being now made new

To bring into the stuff of earth—
Each atom's pattern clear—
Your kingdom, perfect and divine,
Each day a thought more near.

Out in a Melon Patch

I cannot think how watermelons grow.
How is the message coded in the seed
To bring this vine instead of some rank weed
Into the light in its appointed row?
I only scratched the soil to put below
The seed; then sun and rain fulfilled each need
At growing time—a miracle, indeed,
How earth's sure cycles never fail to flow!
I have come now to pick this firm, ripe fruit,
And to anticipate how it will suit
The taste—so juicy, red, and sweet—and pause
To think upon the wonder of the Cause.

A Babysitter's Prayer

Dear God, bless these children in my care. Keep them safe from every harm and stress. Let them feel security with me, even as I feel security in Your care.

Give me of Your wisdom, Father, to meet each problem as it arises. Give me of Your untiring strength and Your unfailing patience. Give me of Your love, that I may pour it out upon these little ones I watch.

Bless me with imagination, that I may devise new games when old ones grow dull. Bless me with insight to see beneath the surface actions to the inner needs of each child. Bless me with calmness and knowledge should an emergency arise.

Gladly I accept the responsibility for these children, knowing You are with me and with them. For Your presence and blessings I give You thanks, and I am happy with my job.

Amen.

Thought - Starter

Do you keep a "cushion" of faith available for use in time of special need, in addition to that which you use every day?

How many men and women do you know who manufacture their own trouble?

Do you think God ever resigns?

Could you get up unselfconsciously, with no advance notice, and open a business meeting with prayer?

Can you name five "basics" of dynamic prayer?

A Prayer

O God, let me not be dulled
into unawareness, insensitivity.
Five senses have You given me;
I would use each one to know
the whole of this, my world.
Let me taste the bitter lemon
as eagerly as the honeycomb,
the bite of the hot chili
as readily as fresh-baked bread.
Let me smell all herb pungencies,
the indefinable odors of old cities,
the musk of irate skunk
before I come to flower fragrances.
Let me feel of the rough tree bark,
finger a satin fabric and homespun,
hold a sea-smoothed pebble, and
(lightly) investigate the locust thorn.
Let me hear all sounds . . .
traffic horn and crowd babble,
bird call and dry grass rustle,
wind howl and sea murmur and child's cry.
O God, let me see, fresh each day
as if newly resurrected, people I love,
the familiar streets I walk upon,
a museum painting, a soaring bridge,
a butterfly wing, an expanse of sky.

Let me learn this earth, this world,
through every sense, new sharpened,
and learning thus, learn Thee.

Departure

A bird held lightly on the hand
Lingers a moment, then is gone . . .
Vibrant wings alive to greet
The morning sun, the dawn.

Just so, a friend that shared
Some miles of this temporal way
Now has taken another turning
To greet a new and radiant day.

A Bond of Hands

I hold out my hand to you . . .
Do you shudder that it is white,
not black like yours?
Is this color, then, to my fault?
Is that color, then, to your praise?
I hold out my hand . . .
Will you take it?

A hand is held out to me . . .
Do I shrink inwardly,
that hand being yellow?
That hand being black?
How shall we forget
the alienation of the past?
How clasp the offered hand?

And yet, our hands do clasp . . .
the white, the black, the yellow.
And who is to know the inner prayer
soundlessly offered
by each of us as our groping fingers
reach . . . and touch . . . and cling?

We are one world.
Take my hand, Brother.

A CELEBRATION OF SEPTEMBER

September Praise

Red is the apple,
And the honey, sweet
From summer's comb;
Golden is the cornstalk,
And fragrant, the late rose.
Now does nature praise Thee,
   God of the growing . . .
   God of the harvesting.
Locust chirr is constant,
Young birds try their wings.
Lightning plays at dusk
Within the storm cloud,
The loose leaf falls with rain.
Now does nature praise Thee,
   God of the seeding . . .
   God of the fruiting time.
And I, too, praise Thee
At the summer's ending,
At autumn's new beginning,
   O God of every beginning . . .
   God of every harvesting.

Creed of a Service - Watcher

I watch service, not clocks, on the job today.

As I do my regular tasks I look at them with a fresh vision to see how I may do a more effective, successful job, thus giving better service.

As I work with others I listen with greater attention to hear the words which may help me on my job. I listen also to hear the word showing me where I may be of service to another.

As I work with my hands I see them as instruments of divine order, doing needed jobs with skill and grace.

Throughout the working day I give added service wherever I can, being quick to go beyond the prescribed limits of my responsibility when there is a need to be met. I watch to see where I might help a co-worker with a kindly word, a smile, a lift on a tedious task.

I watch for service opportunities instead of watching for time to pass. Positioned in God, working for Him in whatever task falls to my willing hands and feet, I would be the leaven to bring increased accomplishment and harmonious relationships into my working environment.

I would be a service-watcher for God.

Commonplaces

If the sparrow,
undistinguished as it is,
be dear to His heart,
then He must surely love
all commonplaces—
the oxeye daisy and the chicory
blooming by the roadside,
the curling brown leaves
that fall before the colors flame,
all puppies and stray kittens,
old lame horses,
and dilapidated barns.
And He must surely, then,
have a special love
for old men who sell newspapers,
for tired, gray mothers,
for janitors and trash collectors,
for salesgirls and typists,
for babies in tenements.
Indeed, He must most surely love
all of us,
don't you think?

After Holidays

Now a pause
to contemplate
new depths
of love,
of brotherhood,
of service;
a taking stock
of useless habits,
thoughtless words,
careless acts;
a resolution
for deepened prayer,
heightened understanding,
broadened brotherhood,
and a new dedication
of my life
to God.

Dedication

I dedicate myself to those ends that will act as a positive force for bringing the victory of peace to all the world. I realize that I have a spiritual responsibility. Knowing and understanding some small part of the one Power and Might which is God, I daily pray that the coming of peace, God's will on earth, may be quickened through me. I pray always that I may be a channel for peace. Through thoughts, words, and actions I resolve to live up to the very best that I know, to be receptive to the guidance of Spirit.

Truly spiritual responsibility is great in these chaotic days. To be equal to the test, I include a period of meditation and prayer in my daily routine. I pray, with many others throughout the whole world, for permanent peace, for cessation of killing and hate, for a great quickening of love over all this earth. I pray that I, as a child of God, may be led to think, say, and do the very best of which I am capable.

In so dedicating myself, I remember that I must be on guard every minute of the twenty-four hours in a day against hatred, prejudice, confusion, selfishness, fear. My thoughts must be kept in tune with peace so that in my own small way I can produce peace on earth. No matter where my work calls, I still think in accordance with my knowledge of truth. My thoughts—as they mirror the love and protection of God—are my shield against any enemy.

Nor are my thoughts alone sufficient. Every word must be in tune with my purpose. I must not utter one negative idea. The least I can do is keep silent if I can find no constructive word. However, it is my duty to see and speak of the good, the true and the real, as opposed to the false conditions of world chaos.

Finally, I dedicate my every action to the bringing about of the establishment and maintenance of lasting peace throughout the world. I do my job, whatever it is, wherever it may lie—on a battlefront or on a homefront—with faith and courage. I know that each small job, multiplied by millions more, is absolutely essential. I search for new ways in which I can be of service to friend, to neighbor, to country. I give unstintingly, willingly, gladly— of myself, my time, my talents, my material possessions, and that spiritual power which is not of me but rather flows through me.

I dedicate myself, my soul and my body, my thoughts, my words, and my deeds to the cause of freedom, to the cause of peace, to the cause of God.

Living Pages

I leave margins of silence
around the activities of day,
letting God write down there
whatever it is He would say.

Then looking backward, I find,
no matter how much *I* revise,
it is in those footnotes
that the heart of my life lies.

Credo

I affirm
Life;
I challenge
Problems;
I accept
Responsibility;
I believe
God;
I live
Today!

The First Fruits

I gladly give God a tenth of all that is mine. As money comes to me I rejoice in the opportunity to give back to God something of His own, counting Him a silent partner in all the affairs of my life. I ask Him to show me where my tithe may be used in His service. I give to God's work and to those organizations ministering in His name. I give to a family in need. I send an inspirational magazine to one whom it may help. I pay my tithe first, then I give thanks as my own portion seems to stretch as I use it, filling my every need.

I give to God in other ways. I give service wherever I can. I give encouragement and inspiration to one who is discouraged. I give love freely and without thought of return. I give a silent blessing to everyone I meet, and I am immeasurably blessed.

I give to God of whatever talent I may have. I develop that talent whether it be the ability to create a home, to teach young eager minds, or to do exacting physical labor. I use it in His service whether it be a humble talent or a dramatic one in some field of art or science. I thank God for it, and as I develop it in love and thankfulness I find in life joyous adventures I have not known before.

God has created an abundance for every man and woman. As I give joyously to God in all these ways, more and ever more of that abundance finds its way into my life. I am blessed and enriched in the intangible things of Spirit as well as in material things.

Thought - Starters

Do you possess spiritual imagination?

Are you a Truth *student* or a Truth *doer*?

What use do you make of routine breaks, such as a wait for an elevator or a telephone call?

How many non-accidents do you suppose there are every day because somebody prayed?

Do you think it is easier for a woman to live a Christ-filled life than it is for a man?

Make Prayer a Live Production

Effective, vital prayer must be a "live production." It must have color, vivid image, perhaps even sound effects. It must, in other words, have emotion behind it.

Effective prayer is the prayer that is real communication between your mind and heart and soul and the one source, God, All-Good. Stereotyped, wordy prayers fail to make that real communication, just as old-time motion pictures shown on television fail to arouse emotion (other than a laugh at their outdated techniques).

So, no matter how brief your prayer is, make it a live, twentieth-century prayer. Phrase it in your own words, feel it with emotion, put yourself into it.

Then give the Receiver a chance to complete the two-way communication. Hold your mind and heart open and alert to catch His response. A conviction, an idea, a phrase, a picture may come to your mind—and that is your answer. Or you may have only a feeling, a feeling of peace or strength or courage or challenge.

Go out, then, and live the answer to your prayer. Make your live prayer a part of the live production that is your life.

Renewal

Fashion a blueprint
for that which you would renew
upon the drawing board of prayer.
Clear the ground for renewal
by letting go
of all that is less than perfect.
Begin to build upon a firm foundation
of the truth that is.
Use the bricks of affirmation,
held by the cement of faith;
follow closely the blueprint
and build joyously.
The challenge of renewal is
the challenge of life.

Job, to the Lord

Whittle me, then,
not into what I am,
rather to fit
what I have no will to be,
yet am destined to suffer
in one long, ambiguous defeat.
The grain goes hard
against the blade.
Hone the double-edge, then,
and whittle me
to some un-final shape.
Leave me
a few rough edges.

Daily Use

Today I look at my life with a penetrating eye. I count my assets, physical and spiritual. I ask myself, "Am I making full and abundant daily use of all that I have?"

Am I giving a pinch-penny tithe to God, or am I giving a full and immediate tenth of the money I receive, giving it joyously to His work? Am I giving some measure of service and talent in His name, without thought of payment?

Am I really aware of the true abundance that is now mine? Do I read the books and wear the clothes, set the table with my best things and enjoy their beauty?

If I feel a lack of material things or of creative ability or of spiritual assets, then consciously, now, today, I begin to build an awareness of abundance in my consciousness. For I do possess abundance and it is the awareness and the acceptance and the daily use that I lack.

I use what I have freely, blessing it, praising God and giving thanks. As I use what I have, more comes; awareness grows; I am in all ways and in all things richly blessed. "Daily use" is a watchword of abundance—material and spiritual.

The Lodestone

There is
within me
that inner
Spirit,
a lodestone
already
magnetized
from my
beginning,
which draws
to my body
health,
to my mind
creativity,
to my soul
the wonder of
life.

A CELEBRATION OF OCTOBER

A Life in the Building

Prayer is the cornerstone
of this, my life—
basic as marrow in the bone
or calm after strife;
basic as breath of air
in the panting lung,
this need, this care
for the song to be sung
to my God, to Him
who has created my being.
By a pseudonym,
perhaps, signing—
this matters no whit.
My life structures grow
if I take care to fit
prayer to God deep below
as the true cornerstone,
basic as blood, basic as bone.

A Spiritual Checklist

Today I ask myself these questions . . .
In a month I shall ask them again, and
If I have used today's answers as a basis
For soul growth, my later answers will show it:

Have I spent even a brief time alone in prayer today?

Have I used brief arrow-prayers for special needs when they arose?

Have I silently given my thanks to God when some good happened?

Have I found somebody to help today, somebody outside my family-friend group?

Have I looked at some stranger and, in silence, recognized Christ in him?

Have I done every job as if God Himself were coming for inspection?

Have I forgiven myself for something I did wrongly, and accepted God's grace?

Have I acted upon intuition, when that intuition followed prayer?

Have I really lived all day long in an active, aware consciousness that God is the one law and the one Mover in my world . . . in all worlds?

A Weekday, a Workday

This, too, is God's day.

Prayer starts this day,
Quiet and serene for a brief time
When I am conditioned
For the hours ahead.
Then I go gladly to work,
Confident, relaxed, unhurried.
The problem becomes a challenge;
The decision is surely made;
The personal relationships
Are rewarding, fruitful ones.
Brief moments of prayer
Intersperse the routine tasks.
The day's work done, I let it go
And find refreshment
In some different activity—
In music, a book, a sport.
Then prayer ends this day,
A day closing as it began.

This, too, is God's day!

Prayer for Achievement

Dear God, help me to begin today to do the work I want to do. The work that fulfills my deep inner desire for self-expression is what I am meant to do—the work that is in accord with Your divine pattern for my life. In it I will find true joy, true happiness, true fulfillment—more in the doing than in any reward that comes from the work. But, doing my right job, I know I will be abundantly blessed with the material needs of my life.

Perhaps the work that lies before me today is not that which my heart desires. I will do it, nevertheless, as well as I am able—finding joy in a job well done. At the same time I will do everything possible to make myself ready for my chosen work. I will study, will read, will practice any needed skills.

Dear God, if I am undecided, help me to know, with a sure inner knowing, what work it is You would have me do. I will listen for Your guidance, will be receptive to the prompting that will let me know which job is right for me.

Let me hesitate no longer. Let me not put off the first steps toward the fulfillment, the deep satisfaction, the lasting joy that come from using my God-given abilities. I would develop each skill, would use it in service and as a blessing to others, knowing that in return I myself will be immeasurably blessed.

Amen.

Manifestation

Take moist clay,
mold to a new shape,
fire:
a ceramic
one-of-a-kind.

Take a thought,
mold in prayer,
fire in action:
a new life,
one-of-a-kind.

Five P's: a Prayer Program

Prepare for prayer. Alone, quiet, turn your whole being away from outer things toward the inner realm of spirit.

Ponder the very essence of God, not asking now, but waiting upon Him, that you may be filled with life, with love, wisdom, joy, abundance.

Picture then, yourself and your life as you desire them, perfectly in accord with God's blueprint for you.

Promise God to do your part in bringing about this perfection of mind, body, and affairs, even as you accept His promises that you are His child, perfect now and always, all things being possible unto you.

Perform now, in thought, in word, in outer action, as if you were indeed His child, and already manifesting the perfection that is the Truth.

Credo for Exploration

I believe
In the far vision and the fearless spirit,
In the valiant journey to new worlds,
In the faith that is life's guiding star.

I believe
In the leadership that inspires followers,
In the patience that can wait for victory,
In the courage that is never defeated.

I believe
In new, undiscovered worlds of the spirit,
In the men and women now pioneering,
In the prayer and praise that bring discovery.
Oh, I believe in victory of the spirit
Wherever the way may lead!

Take a Prayer Break

Take a prayer break today. It need not be *instead* of a coffee break, although it may be. It could easily be *in addition to*, for a prayer break depends more on desire than on time. You need not leave your desk, your lathe, your drafting board. You need only turn, ever so briefly, your attention from the outer things to the inner, to complete momentarily your own personal connection with God.

A word of warning (or of encouragement): the prayer break easily becomes a strong habit. Once you become used to turning often to God during the day, you will continue to do so, for you will experience a wonderful new sense of security as you rely on divine guidance to help with each problem of the day.

Do you need to speak to an employee whose work has been slipping? That minute between asking your secretary to send the employee in, and his arrival, is all you need for a prayer break in which you ask God for the right words to say. Have you a need to master a new machine shop technique? A prayer break before you begin will give you faith in God's ever-present help and faith in your own God-given ability to learn. Do you have a stack of letters to tackle late in the afternoon when you are already tired? A prayer break will refresh your mind as well as your spirit.

For meeting the day's problems as they arise, such an unspoken prayer as this is sufficient: "Dear God, this is my problem . . . Thank You for Your help, Your wisdom, Your strength. Amen."

The prayer break can serve a long-range purpose,

too. Perhaps there is a personality trait you would like to overcome, a habit from which you wish to be free, or a chronic-type problem. An affirmation prayer can help.

Take time to find or to write an affirmation expressing your problem in positive terms. State the Truth, the basic reality, and give thanks for its present perfect manifestation in you. Try affirmations such as these: *"I praise and give thanks for an abundance of God's supply present here and now to fulfill my every need." "I am filled with divine confidence as God-in-me performs this task perfectly."*

Use an affirmation custom-built to fit your need. Write it on a card and tuck it in your wallet or put it on your desk. In every prayer break use that affirmation. You will soon know it by mind and heart; you will soon know it by soul. In fact, you will soon be realizing it in outward manifestation in your life.

Experiment with the prayer break idea. Use it to keep that wonderful sense of oneness with God that is sometimes difficult to maintain in the rush of daily living. Use it to solve the problem of the moment. Use it to progress spiritually toward the goal of Christhood. Use it to expand spiritual horizons, and physical horizons will widen until they encompass the whole of this vast universe.

Add a prayer break to your mental schedule of the day. You will reap rich dividends in health and strength, in inner poise and outer development, in spiritual growth, and in outer achievement of success.

Prayer for a New Business

Father-God, we ask You now to be a partner with us in this new venture—but not a silent partner. We would have You speak into our mind and heart the guidance and the inspiration that we need.

We feel there is a true need that this new business will help to fill. Help us to meet that need most effectively, giving service, giving goods in overflowing measure, and giving an added premium—Your blessing—in every transaction.

Our cornerstone is faith: faith in You, faith in those whom we will serve, and faith in ourself. Help us ever to expand this threefold faith. Only with inner growth can we expect outer growth in material things.

As we look to You today and in the days to come for help and guidance, so are we determined to share our success with You. We will acknowledge Your presence here; we will put Your share of profits into work that is dedicated to You. We will look to You for daily help to meet each new problem as it arises; we will give You thanks for that constant help each day.

Be ever with us, Father-God, today as we launch this new business, and in all the tomorrows as our business grows.

On Having Roots

All the strong things have roots:
the great mahoganies buttressed
against the slashing of hurricane winds,
the ever-flowing Amazon reaching seaward
from the wellsprings of the Andes,
the spirit of a free and freedom-loving people
growing out of a history of striving,
and the man who stands firm
no matter what the winds that buffet him—
no matter who may landslide from him.
So let the roots of your faith
grow deeply, strongly, in the fertile soil
of all the universal truths, nourished
by prayer and growing in meditation
and strengthened as you live by trust.
All the strong things have their roots.

That Ship of Yours

Don't just wait for your ship to come in. Go to meet it! Maybe you'll have to start in a rowboat; perhaps you already have a good start and are making way in a motorboat. Even if you have to swim, make a start. (The Panama Canal has been transited by swimmers as well as by battleships and luxury liners.)

Do something, with what you have, toward what you want. Chart a course to follow, and navigate by prayer. Don't mark time on the shore and wish for your ship. Take yourself in hand; know that your inmost desires are prompted by God's plan for your life.

Go out to meet your ship!

Identity

Who am I?
I am he or she
   who can become
   the man or the woman
   I dream of being.
My dreams are dreams
   that I intend
   to make into reality.
I work to solve
   each problem of today
   so that tomorrow's challenge
   will lead to greater achievement.
Who am I?
I am a child of God.

The Golden Harvest

Autumn is the season of the harvest's golden beauty. Then row on row of gallant cornstalks march across the land in full array. Barns nearly burst with sweet dried hay. The golden harvest moon rides high. Nature lays her plenty out as if the loving Father had brought forth His whole abundant store and said, "See, my doubting prodigal, there is enough for all to share."

There is a golden harvest of the spirit, too, when wisdom is mellowed by experience, when love has gone beyond small selfish bounds to know an infinite horizon, when patience and humility are paired with dreams, God-given, and the means, God-given also, of bringing them to fulfillment. Such a climax in the life of any man can bring—and does bring—God's kingdom closer to the earth.

The harvest's golden beauty, burnished bright, shines forth across a great and growing land; shines out in radiance and in love from the face of man.

A CELEBRATION OF NOVEMBER

Formula for Achievement

It takes a proper combination of factors,
In a life as in a business,
To bring the success of achievement.
I must be my own "quality product,"
A product constantly being upgraded
Through prayer-communication with God,
And maintained in a faith-and-service
Relationship with men and women about me.
I must manage my life effectively,
Learning to make decisions
(Prayer-guided decisions they must be),
And then acting immediately with faith.
My talents, my resources must be
Put to full and profitable use,
Bringing dividends of personal joy,
Dividends of growing fulfillment.
My accounting system is geared to giving—
The giving of full measure of myself
In prayer, in service, in work.
The savings I list are those of time,
Of energy, of effectiveness when I learn
To look only forward, each day.
And the profits? Total abundance
Of every material and spiritual good!

Homage to November

Sing praise to November!
The farmer's harvest safe
within the bulging bin and mow;
the jelly ruby in the jar;
the garden produce proudly counted
in the quart, the pint, the frozen box;
the leaf-fall finished
and the migrant birds all flown.
Now watch the sun rise later
and fall earlier to darkness
in late November afternoon.
Now take time to savor
the aftermath of harvest,
to cheer the football hero,
and to think again of Pilgrim folk
sharing the fruits of their new world
with Indian brothers and giving thanks
for the richness of this land.
Sing praise to November!

Watch Fob of the Mind

Divine Mind in my mind. This is the watch fob, the watch chain that can guard and protect the mind.

The mind is constantly (at least during waking hours) ticking out thoughts. These thoughts create one's individual environment—his life. Each thought goes forth to produce its own effect in body and affairs.

Divine Mind in my mind. Although other phrases could serve, this seems to be a chain of words that makes a perfect watch fob. Each word is a strong link; the whole is a powerful chain to guard the mind within from the subtle, negative influences of the material world.

To begin each day by placing these words consciously in the mind is to make an affirmative start. The human mind is linked firmly to Divine Mind—the omniscient One. This can easily be a brief, added part—an enrichment of the morning meditation.

In the days when a watch fob was a mark of social standing, a gentleman must surely have been subconsciously aware of this small chain and whatever ornament he cared to place upon it. The modern-day Truth student who wears a mental watch fob will ever be consciously aware of it. Because this awareness may be in large part completely beneath the outer, busy level of the brain, the watch fob will be a special safeguard against the little negative pilferers, the subliminal attacks on consciousness.

And during the day, from time to time, the wearer of this mental chain will perhaps direct his conscious thought to it, polishing it with prayerful concern, with deepening understanding of its real meaning.

Divine Mind in my mind. With these words guarding your thought processes, creative words will flow forth to create in their likeness a more perfect body, a more harmonious world, a manifestation of increasing abundance.

Safe - Conduct Pass

Prayer is the perfect "safe-conduct pass" through life. Were it not for faith, each day might become a hazardous journey; at home, traveling, at work there are dangers, yet so seldom do things go wrong that normally we expect no trouble.

When prayer is the key to the day and the lock to the night, as an old proverb puts it, then faith shines brightly. The affairs of the day move forward safely, harmoniously. Health and happiness, achievement and prosperity are the certain by-products of using this particular safe-conduct pass—regular and constant prayer, morning and night and in-between.

With a close and growing relationship with God, achieved through prayer, life is an exciting challenge, a safe journey through the years.

The Gift

This is my day for giving.
I give away love with breakfast,
encouragement with the good-byes
as the family divides into the day.
I give care and service
to home and car, to job or to jobs,
as they swim past me in the stream
of the flowing hours.
I give away silent blessings
embellished with smiles
to friend and stranger . . . but who
can be a stranger, inwardly,
when we are all one in God?
I give away all sorts of things:
letters and clippings and poems,
cookies and paper clips and used stamps.
I give away what is not mine to give,
but God's . . . all is His.
Today is my day for giving.
Every day is my day for giving!

Thought - Starters

Do you think improved advertising could make Christian beliefs a more effective force in the world today?

Is there a common denominator of all faiths?

Can you formulate an equation for man's relationship to God?

A recent filler quotation in a newspaper: "It was never loving that emptied the heart, nor giving that emptied the purse." Do you believe this?

Do you ever consider recreation in terms of spiritual re-creation?

Appointment

My first appointment is with God.
No matter how my daybook reads,
I talk with Him the first of all.
Then, all day long, it seems my needs
For strength and courage, patience, time
Are met; and when I make a choice
Or face some grave decision's test
I'm aided by a silent Voice,
An inner knowing what to do.
The business prospers; I do, too.

The Pattern

There is a perfect pattern for my life. As I look to God for guidance, as I act on the feeling or lead that comes, then my life begins to unfold in marvelous ways. Every chance for achievement, every opportunity for service and fulfillment is mine.

It is only when I am off the beam, not going in accordance with the divine pattern, that frustration, bitterness, and failure are mine.

But no matter in what state my life now appears, I can begin today to take the first step toward getting in step with the pattern. It is so simple—prayer and faith, then action on the guidance I receive from God. It may seem that all doors are swinging shut; then I must look for the one door that remains open. That will be the one leading to the fulfillment of every dream, for it will be the one that fits the pattern.

As I begin to follow the pattern that is mine, and mine alone, all goodness comes into my life. The very cells of my body take up new life, new strength, a new perfection in their functioning. Unlimited supply, such as I have not dreamed of, is mine. My heart is alive with a new joy of living, but calm and secure with the peace of God. Harmonious relationships, new rewarding friendships—all sorts of wonderful happenings come into my life.

Yes, today I begin to live according to the perfect pattern for my life.

A Triple Play

Cultivate
that inner atmosphere
in which prayer can flourish.

Communicate
with God, both listening
and speaking in a dialogue
of praise and practicality.

Motivate
the sum total of your life,
the business hours,
the off-work hours,
in the affirmative directions
in which these daily dialogues
direct.

I Prepare My Heart

For the day of Thanksgiving I now prepare my heart. In prayer I seek cleansing of faults that clutter up my soul—impatience, intolerance, irritation, resentment. I seek cleansing of bitterness, envy, and resentment that may be buried deep, almost out of my knowledge. I let all these things go now, never to hold me down again! I will be free of all negative thinking and saying and doing.

Cleansed, I fill my heart and mind and soul with divine love and let it flow forth in every thought and word and action. I am an open channel for great joy which lifts me to new spiritual heights. I become freshly aware of God's world about me. I see it filled with beauty, with abundance, with life. It is not static; it is a world teeming with creative activity. The one Life is constantly being manifested in my life.

Oh, I am renewed as I prepare for Thanksgiving! My body is quickened with new life and strength. I see with a new vision. I hear and smell with a new keenness. I feel with a fresh touch. I am a child of God; this is His world; all is vibrant with His life and ready to give Him thanks!

"Direct your heart to the Lord, and serve Him only." I prepare now for Thanksgiving, in my heart.

Thanksgiving Credo

I believe
in the giving of joyous thanks to God:
thanks for shelter and for food,
thanks for sun and wind and rain,
thanks for family and for friends,
thanks for a job that only I can do,
thanks for beauty in every form,
thanks for happiness and fun.
I believe
in thanksgiving as a form of prayer,
of affirmation of the Truth, and so
I believe
in the giving of joyous thanks to God:
thanks for perfection of the mind,
thanks for perfection of the body,
thanks for the challenge of problems,
thanks for the effort of creative activity,
thanks for the perfect manifestation
of God in every part of my life.
And I do so give Him thanks today.

Hymn of Thanksgiving

Here stands a city: any city, in any country,
in any world, in any universe, any galaxy.
Hear, O Lord, a hymn of praise and thanksgiving
rising, rising—upward, outward, inward the curve.
The bins are piled with the plenty of creation
chosen by mind after mind after mind to be known
in the multiplicity of the ever-present harvest.
Hear, O Lord, a hymn of praise and thanksgiving
manifesting, growing, changing, transmuting.
The torch flame of freedom, no candle's flame
but a brilliant shaft of energy, is unquenchable.
The light is from everlasting to everlasting.
Hear, O Lord, a hymn of praise and thanksgiving
echoing and re-echoing with the harmonies of light
in the patterns of light at the speed of light
throughout the eternities of Thy creation of light.
O Lord, let us too hear Thy hymn of light;
let us see Thy praise in light; let us, in the end,
be Thy light, forever and ever shining. Amen.

Litany for Light

The Lord is my light!
He is the light of all my days:
Let rain fall—hail, snow;
Let the atomic fog envelop earth.
Still the Lord is my light.
He brightens all my days.

The Lord is my light!
He is the light of my whole body.
With light He casts out shadows, imperfections;
For where He shines there can be no darkness.
The Lord is my healing light.
He radiates perfection in my body.

The Lord is my light!
He is the light of this, my mind:
So is erased the darkness of depression;
So is swept away negation.
Always is the Lord my light.
He illumines every thought I think.

The Lord is my Light!
He is the light of lights within my soul.
Through meditation, faith, and prayer,
He leads me to the glory of His very presence.
The Lord is my Light.
The Lord is, indeed, my light and my salvation!

A CELEBRATION OF DECEMBER

Meditation

Now do I look to Christ:
    Christ beneath
    and Christ above,
    Christ behind
    and Christ before me.

Now do I feel the Christ
    healing with love,
    guiding with wisdom,
    calming with peace,
    being belief.

Now do I find Christ Himself
    within and without
    in the thought
    and in the word,
    deeply embedded in the prayer
    and outwardly expressed
    in the action of life.

Now do I see Christ;
Now do I know Him;
Now do I rest in Him;
Now am I born anew in Him. Amen.

Prayer Circle

Have you ever stood in a quiet twilight and thrown a pebble into the still waters of an icy mountain lake? Have you watched as the pebble produced its first circle, then another and another? A prayer should be like that tiny pebble, producing its first reaction in your own soul, in the innermost recesses of your mind and heart, and then gradually widening its effect until it embraces all earth and heaven.

In the stillness of your mind, begin your prayer. Bless your body; let the healing forces flow freely through every cell of it, raising it surely, steadily to perfection. Make no attempt to heal specific ills; rather see the oneness, the wholeness of your body. Be not ashamed of your body. Be proud of it! Let it radiate the glory of its perfection.

Widen the circle of your prayer to include those nearest to you in spirit—family, friends, home, and work. See all filled with joy; see them prospering in the things of earth and the things of heaven. Feel your oneness with those you love who are far away. Place them fearlessly and freely in God's care, knowing them to be guarded, upheld, and divinely led by the same Spirit that leads you into still waters of peace. Bless your home and your work with the harmony and divine efficiency of Spirit.

Your prayer circle will grow as you include every acquaintance in your blessing, knowing that for each there is only one presence and one power, that each is a perfect expression of the one great God force. Let this harmonizing flow of Spirit free your mind from every trace of prejudice, faultfinding, or resentment.

Bless the land where you live. See the great Spirit of divine wisdom, justice, and love hovering over it to protect and guide it. Know that those who lead and govern are divinely inspired, that they are strengthened so that they may bear their responsibilities easily, know that they are guided in making every decision.

Finally the circle of your prayer will widen until it has no conscious limits. The Spirit of the one Mind, God, spreads over the whole world. Peace and love are the only realities. Every intolerance must go. There is no room for evil, for untruth, when this great force for good reaches out and out through a prayer begun in a human heart.

The circle of good animated through your prayer does not stop. It can never stop, but reaches on, spreads ever wider, in every direction, until it embraces all of earth and all of heaven.

Prayer on a Streetcorner

Here on a busy streetcorner, Father, I am one with You. I see You in countless active forms: I see You in action as a policeman directs traffic, as a taxi driver assists an elderly passenger, as a newsboy hawks his papers. I see You in all the hurry and the bustle.

I feel the rhythm of Your harmony in the swift flow of traffic, the graceful lift of a cathedral's spire, the joyous lilt of a teen-ager's walk.

Father, bless each one who passes by. Wipe out the doubt and fear that bring the tense walk and the furrowed forehead. Heal the imperfection of mind as well as of body, of all those now in need. Spread forth the harmony of Truth and let it find a welcome in every heart and mind that is receptive at this moment.

Bless this busy corner. Make it hallowed by awareness of Your presence here. My own thoughts turn to You, knowing even in confusion the joy of communion with You, feeling the warmth of enfolding love, the strength of power, the guiding arrow of Your wisdom.

Thank You, God, for the blessings of this moment.

Consciousness of Health

Today I begin to build a new consciousness of health. I acknowledge radiant health as my God-given heritage. I claim this inheritance today.

I accept as true this perfection of body, regardless of appearances. I praise and give thanks for the life in every cell, for the cooperation between these cells, for the amazing inherent power of renewal and regrowth. I rejoice in a perfect body. Throughout the day I praise my body silently, knowing that the inner Christ Spirit directs and superintends its working. I release quickly any thought of disease or malfunctioning. I know and affirm the truth of health.

I build a consciousness of life, health, perfection. Gone are fears and tensions—they have no place in such a consciousness! I give frequent thanks for the life manifesting in my body, perfecting and renewing it. I praise the healing, renewing forces at work in my body. I feel the deep inner quickening which accompanies the realization of wholeness.

I praise the perfection of my body. I call forth health and perfection through prayer and praise, through affirmation and thanksgiving. I build a strong, enduring consciousness of perfect health. I claim my heritage of life!

Plea

Christ,
save me
from darkness
of prejudice,
eclipse of Your light;
it is Yourself I shame
when I fail to see You in
a man who does not share
my skin's color or
my custom, for
we are one
in You,
Christ.

Commentary

A minute
is eternity
translated
into the now;
a prayer,
the impossible
transmuted
to possibility;
thanksgiving
is joy
crystallized;
love
is God
known.

The Gift of Talents

Talents are God-given abilities. I rejoice in each talent I possess. I work to develop each one and know it is given me to use in service. At first, as I study and practice to develop my skill, I may not see any need in the world, in my world, for this particular gift. It may even seem self-indulgent to use time and perhaps money in developing my talent. However, if I feel truly led to develop this talent, I know that God desires me to do so. When I am ready, opportunity for its use in a way that will bring joy and fulfillment both to others and myself will appear.

Having developed and used one or several talents in my life, I rejoice at the opportunity to develop still another. This may be a talent of which I was not even previously aware.

Life and growth—are they not almost synonymous? I go steadily forward, developing new talents and using old ones in new ways. So do I give joy and service; so do I reap a rich harvest of love and joy, satisfaction and success.

I develop and use every talent I possess. I give thanks for these God-given abilities every day of my life. "Having gifts that differ according to the grace given to us, let us use them."

Thought - Starters

What would be the five most important steps to take if you embarked on a program of personal spiritual development?

Is mind expansion a valid goal?

When you know your schedule is full, can you say "No" without feeling guilty if you are asked to do one more public-service job?

Have you ever received spiritual guidance in a dream?

How many nonessentials could you cut from your daily schedule to give you time for unhurried prayer?

The Giving Season

The spirit of giving fills my heart this Christmas season.

Christmas *is* the giving season, and this year I remember the spiritual gifts as well as the material ones.

With every Christmas card I send a blessing. I span the miles with a thought of love and thankfulness for friendship as I seal the envelopes. As I add the postage stamps I breathe a prayer to God to bring each one the inner gifts of the Spirit this year—a deeper understanding of Truth, a closer communion with God, a growing ability to express divine love, joy, and peace.

With every Christmas gift I wrap a prayer that this Christmas season will be filled with spiritual meaning for the receiver. As I tie the ribbons I breathe a prayer to God to grant to this one his dearest wish, to fill his most heartfelt need.

With all my gifts I send God's blessings. I wrap each one round with my own love and with the blessing of divine love.

The spirit of giving fills my heart this Christmas season!

Before Christmas

Already
the Three Kings
are journeying
toward the Star
toward the Child
toward love.

A Stained - Glass Window

Light shining through a stained-glass window makes a beautiful, glowing picture. The colors are vivid, radiant. The figures are shining. So should each person let the very light of God shine through him.

Jesus Christ in His conscious unity with God did indeed shine with a wondrous light. And He said, "You are the light of the world." Because we know the Christ within, that same light can shine through us. We can keep the panes of the window that is our life clean and shining through faith in God; through prayer we can receive the guidance which will harmonize our life so that the light, shining through, will form a picture of beauty. We can be alert to wipe away any doubt, fear, anxiety . . . any lack of faith in God's goodness and complete power . . . that would veil the light as it shines through.

Let us know this radiant light as the very healing power of God, able to perfect any ill and fill any lack whatsoever. Let us praise God for it and rejoice as it shines through us each day.

A stained-glass window is a rare work of art; so also is a life filled with the very light of God.

Christmas Gift

This Christmas I would light a candle
In some forlorn child's eyes;
Place a new star of friendship
In someone's lonely skies.
I would put a sparkling wreath of joy
Where it might melt a bitter heart;
Be steadfast in my prayer for peace
For all the world, not just a part.
So in this season, love-beguiled,
Would I gift the little Christ Child.

Kaleidoscope

Hold to your eye
the colors of Christmas:
flame of poinsettia, holly's red,
spicy greens and the candles' glow,
bright papers and ribbons,
a hundred cards,
and a cathedral's hushed, dim nave.

Hold to your ear
the sounds of the season:
Christmas carols from a dozen lands,
joyous bells and their pealing,
organ and choir and a child's high voice,
the silence of snowfall late at night.

Hold to your heart, O hold to your heart
the unchanging dream of Christmas:
the shining Star that led Wise Men on
to a Babe in his mother's arms,
and, all about, the angels praying
as we must pray, as we all must pray,
"Peace on earth; good will to all men."

The Christmas Light

Radiant, the holy singing light
Streams forth to bless on Christmas night
With some new pulse of energy . . .
Or is it only that we see
With clearer vision at this time
When we have always seen the sign
Of Christ, the Baby, born again
Within the seeking hearts of men?
This is the light that blazed the sky
When shepherds scanned the heavens high
Above their flock-filled greening hills
And heard the angels sing their trills
Of glorious glad tidings sent
Unto all men, that God had spent
The price of His own dear-loved Son
Forevermore to teach the one
Commandment, teach the law of love.
Oh, let us look, not high above
In starry skies, this Christmas night,
But in our hearts, for the Christmas light.

Christmas Credo

I believe
in the birth of the baby Jesus
two thousand years ago.
Wrapped in swaddling clothes
and lying in a manger, He was adored
by shepherds and by kings, who found Him
spotlighted by a star.
I believe
in the Christmastime rebirth
in every human heart and soul
of love and joy and peace,
heralded by the star of faith.
I believe
in the very presence of the Christ,
God's constant Christmas gift,
enshrined within men's hearts.
I believe
in Christmas.

Extensions of Christmas

Star-shine
    an infinity
    of light
love
    radiating
    into myriad
    relationships
music
    the sound
    the silence
    echoing
    in the heart
    and finally the
gift
    which is
life

The Flame of Spirit

A light shining
in every man,
burning steadily
when the wick
is trimmed
by prayer,
burning most purely
in atmosphere
of faith, love
and joy,
but shining still
in darkest night
of the soul—
the flame of spirit
cannot be put out
for it was lit
by God.

Litany

Dear Lord, I wait upon Thee:
   Fill me with perfect life.
Dear Lord, I wait upon Thee:
   Fill me with renewed strength.
Dear Lord, I wait upon Thee:
   Fill me with inner vision.
Dear Lord, I wait upon Thee:
   Fill me with a deep quietness.
Dear Lord, I wait upon Thee:
   Fill me with vibrant harmony.
Dear Lord, I wait upon Thee:
   Fill me with radiant love.

Dear Lord, here am I:
   Fill me to overflowing with Thyself.

                     Amen.

After the End

The way out is the way in. The way in is the way out.
    way   way
      out   the
        is   is
          the   in
             way   way
               in. The
             way   way
          the   in
        is   is
     out   the
way   way
The way out is the way in. The way in is the way out.

190

PRINTED U.S.A.

110F-15M-11-70

Kippur) is to highlight both our need and our ability to effect our own atonement.

In classic Christianity, sin is a condition in which one is born. Baptism removes the original sin, but it does not remove future sins of people who are sinful by nature and who can be saved only by a change in their nature. That change cannot take place without help, however. Jesus is the source of that help. His death on the cross was a vicarious atonement for all sinful people, past and future. Only faith in Jesus makes salvation possible.

In Judaism, the responsibility for improving life and attaining goodness rests upon the individual. In Christianity, the individual is helpless without the Christ. In Judaism, there can be no intermediary between God and people; each individual must confront the Creator directly. In classic Christianity, Jesus is the intermediary. (And there are other intermediaries as well, such as priests, who are thought to be the direct successors of the Apostles.)

Judaism makes no dichotomy between flesh and spirit. It regards both as good, since both come from the Creator. It follows that sex is viewed as an expression of love channeled through marriage, not as a base animal instinct. Eating gives us an opportunity to strengthen the body; it is not just a biological necessity. Poverty is not esteemed as a means to greater piety, but is viewed as an unfortunate fact that must be remedied.

Historical Christianity, on the other hand, contrasts impurity of the flesh to purity of the soul. The soul should free itself from the physical as much as possible. Virginity, celibacy, and poverty are highly desirable states. Christian saints were those who succeeded in freeing themselves from physical desires and worldly concerns. The most righteous Jews, on the other hand, were recognized as having channeled their physical natures into ways of actively improving human conditions caused by the ills of society.

Both Judaism and Christianity insist upon monotheism. But

Jewish faith rests upon the uncompromising oneness and uniqueness of God. Christianity teaches the doctrine of the Trinity, of the one God consisting of three elements or aspects. Judaism believes that no power exists independent of God; neither Satan nor any supernatural being constitutes an independent force that can oppose or defy God. In contrast, historical Christianity and some present-day denominations believe in Satan as the power of evil which functions independently of God.

The two religions differ in their appraisal of miracles. In Judaism, miracles play a secondary role. The postbiblical rabbis often endeavored to provide rational explanations for miracles recorded in Scripture. Were all stories of miracles completely removed, Judaism would not be altered in any way. Christianity, on the other hand, assigns them prominence. Much is made of the miracles ascribed to Jesus. Miracles were also ascribed to many saints. Any attempt to eliminate miracles in Christianity would radically alter the very nature of its historical tradition.

Judaism assumes faith in God, and then leaves it to the individual. No assembly of religious authorities can vote to declare what may or may not be believed. What has been central to the Jewish tradition is correct conduct. Proper *behavior,* ritual and moral, is the most essential element. If people truly believe in a God of love and righteousness, it will be reflected in their behavior. Christianity stresses correct *belief.* It insists that one can be saved by faith. Authoritative bodies have met to formulate specific articles of belief. Judaism, of course, has also been concerned with faith, as Christianity has been concerned with deeds, but they have differed in their emphases.

Thus, although both religions accept the Hebrew Scriptures as sacred, and although they share the moral imperatives flowing from faith in one God, they differ in many fundamental conceptions of humanity and in many outlooks on life. These differences need not imply hostility or competition. They indicate two different approaches to the same goal, that of making God truly sovereign in the world. Each should attempt to understand the other without seeking to lure the adherents of one into the camp of the other. Both Jews and Christians need to live in conformity with the holiest teachings of their respective faiths, while demonstrating in thought and in deed what they hold in common. If they do, they will be testifying to the strength of their convictions and to the validity of their faiths.

Suggested Readings for Further Study

Sandmel, Samuel, *The Genius of Paul* (New York: Farrar, Straus and Cudahy, 1958)

————, *We Jews and Jesus* (London and New York: Oxford University Press, 1965)

Weiss-Rosmarin, Trude, *Judaism and Christianity: The Differences* (New York: Jonathan David, 1965)

ADDITIONAL SUGGESTIONS

Bokser, Ben Zion, *Judaism and the Christian Tradition* (New York: Burning Bush Press, 1967)

Gordis, Robert, *Judaism in a Christian World* (New York: McGraw Hill, 1966)

Greenstone, Julius H., *The Messiah Idea in Jewish History* (Philadelphia: The Jewish Publication Society, 1943)

Littel, Franklin H., *The Crucifixion of the Jews* (New York: Harper and Row, 1975)

Samuel, Maurice, *You Gentiles* (New York: Harcourt, Brace and Company, 1924)

Schoeps, Hans Joachim, *The Jewish-Christian Argument* (London: Faber and Faber, 1963)

Silver, Abba Hillel, *Where Judaism Differs* (New York: MacMillan Company, 1956)

————, *A History of Messianic Speculations in Israel* (Boston: Beacon Press, 1959)

CHAPTER 13

A Personal Story of Conversion

RACHEL COWAN

*G*ROWING up in Wellesley, Massachusetts, a wealthy suburban community populated largely by white Protestants, I always assumed that I would raise my own children in a New England colonial house such as my ancestors had built. It would be on the side of a hill, shaded by leafy maples and apple trees in the summer, and surrounded by brilliant foliage in the fall. At Christmas we would cut our own tree, bake cookies, and put two candles in each window.

Today I am raising my children in a tenth-floor apartment on the Upper West Side of Manhattan. My husband and I have furnished it comfortably and eclectically. Prominent on our walls are paintings with Jewish themes; our bookcases house many volumes of books on Jewish subjects. Every Friday night we light Shabbat candles and recite *berakhot* over wine and *ḥallah* before dinner. At Ḥanukkah, each of the four of us lights his own *menorah*. On the last night, thirty-two candles shine out toward the neighbors in the building across the street.

My path to Judaism has taken me far from that New England hillside, but has brought me the sense of history and the feeling for place that I longed for as a child, and much more. It took me many years to decide to convert, but now I feel deeply rooted in Judaism. History, tradition, and a growing faith in God have given more meaning to my life than I ever imagined I would find.

Looking back at the lengthy process of conversion, I see several stages of development. As a child I was deeply influenced by my parents' humanism. They taught me early that one of my responsibilities in life is to fight prejudice and discrimination. They gave me *The Diary of Anne Frank* to read, and I always felt that she was a friend to whose memory I had to be loyal. I often felt I was defending her when I argued against the ignorant anti-Semitic ideas of my classmates. I knew no Jews in Wellesley, for there was a restrictive covenant preventing the sale of houses to them, but I had Jewish friends at summer camp and at college. They never discussed religion, however, so I knew very little about Judaism. Nevertheless, when I fell in love with Paul Cowan, I liked the fact that he was Jewish. I hoped he would be able to teach me something about Jewish traditions. He, however, had grown up in such an assimilated Jewish family that he knew nothing about any Jewish holidays.

My family attended the Unitarian Church in Wellesley, where I was active in the youth group and taught Sunday School. I agreed with the liberal ideas that the minister preached, and I loved the music and the beauty of the Christmas and Easter services. Once I met Paul, though, I thought it would be preferable to raise our children as Jews rather than as Unitarians, for they would have such a magnificent history to feel part of and such a rich culture to participate in. I also felt responsible to help maintain the chain of Jewish generations whose links had never been broken.

But it never occurred to me to convert when I married Paul. He barely knew any more about Judaism than I did, and it seemed unfair to expect *me* to convert if *he* didn't have to. Besides, nobody raised the issue with us. I knew I wanted to know more about Judaism, but that seemed like a project for us both to work on together.

If we were going to raise our children as Jews, we needed to learn many things. We didn't even know how to light a Ḥanukkah *menorah*. We asked friends to lead a Passover *Seder* for us, and to teach us how to light candles on Friday night. With a group of parents we started a weekly after-school Jewish learning center for the kids (the *Ḥavurah* School). Working on the curriculum with the teachers, we learned a great deal.

During those years I saw myself as a fellow-traveler. I felt that our family life was enriched and strengthened by the rituals we were beginning to incorporate into our life. I was proud of what our children were learning, and glad that Paul was coming to understand more about what being Jewish means, and what it meant to him. I enjoyed the things we were doing and felt lucky to be able to participate, but I never thought I would become Jewish. It was clear to me that one was Jewish either by virtue of birth and a shared cultural history, or because of a religious commitment. But no matter how good my *latkes, ḥallah,* or *gefilte* fish tasted, I would never have Jewish genes, or know what it was like to grow up Jewish. Furthermore, I did not consider myself a religious person. Therefore a conversion, which implied to me the taking on of a new faith, seemed to be out of the question.

It was important to me that the Jewish community we lived in regarded me as an integral part. Once, on our honeymoon, Paul and I had traveled in Israel. We met with sharp criticism from Israelis who learned that I was not Jewish. That was the first time I had been the object of prejudice, and it hurt. It made us wary of getting close to any organized Jewish group.

Several years after we started the *Ḥavurah* School, a group of parents and teachers began to meet once a month to read the Torah in English and to discuss what we read. We then began to enclose the discussion in a very abbreviated worship service. Paul and I also began to attend High Holy Day services conducted by a group of young Jews in the neighborhood. They met in a very crowded apartment, and shared leadership of the service. For several years I barely understood what was happening, but I liked the spirit, the singing, and the English text for the meditations. I began to look forward to *Rosh Hashanah,* and joined with Paul in fasting on *Yom Kippur.*

Then a terribly sad thing happened to our family. Paul's parents were both killed in a fire in their apartment. The horror and sadness of their death was made bearable for us by the *Havurah* community, who really took care of us. They brought us food, they took care of our children, they sat and talked with us. We had never heard of the Jewish tradition of mourning, sitting *shivah,* but they taught us what to do, and we found it comforting.

In the months after the fire, I found myself looking forward more eagerly to our worship services. In trying to make sense of my in-laws' lives and their deaths, I unexpectedly found myself struggling with questions of faith.

Over the next two years, I took several classes—one on the Book of Exodus, one on the Prophets, and one on Kabbalah. I discovered that Jewish study was fascinating. Our family visited Israel for six weeks. This time I felt at home there, and loved the country despite its many problems.

One day I realized that I felt very differently about converting. What had formerly seemed impossible now seemed totally natural. It was clear to me that Judaism would be the spiritual path I would follow, and that the Jewish community felt like home.

I still was troubled, however, by the question of what converting to Judaism implied about my relationship to my parents and siblings. I did not want to participate in a procedure which implied that my family background was not adequate, or that I had to reject who I was in order to become somebody new. Some Jewish texts are very negative about converts' origins, and I didn't want to do something that subscribed to that attitude. When I married Paul, a teacher of mine once said, I did not give up my past. Rather, I brought all my strengths to the new relationship. The same would be true of becoming Jewish. I would not be bringing Christian religious beliefs into my new faith, but I would bring to my new role as a Jew the strengths I had acquired as a person, many of them taught by my parents.

As Paul and I learned more and more about Judaism, we came to observe more Jewish practices. We stopped working on the Sabbath (Saturday), stopped going out on Friday nights, stopped eating the foods that were specifically forbidden in the Bible. For me, it was important to understand something about each new law before I observed it. I couldn't take them all on at once.

As I began to look for rabbis to supervise my conversion, I reaffirmed my belief that I could take on Jewish observance only gradually. I finally realized that I felt most comfortable as a Conservative Jew, not as an Orthodox one. The attitude to women in Orthodox Judaism was also an important factor, because I had learned about Judaism from people who believed that women should participate equally in all aspects of the service, and I valued that practice highly.

It was emotionally difficult for me to meet with many rabbis, trying to find those who would accept my decision and agree to serve on a *bet din* to supervise my conversion. It was both puzzling and painful to have to knock on so many doors, only to be told that my understanding of being Jewish was not appropriate for their standards. When I finally decided that I would have a Conservative conversion, a close friend who is a rabbi found two other rabbis who readily agreed to participate in the *bet din*.

The idea of the *mikvah* made me feel anxious. For one thing, I associated it with baptism, an idea I had always resisted. Of course I soon realized that baptism was derived from the *mikvah*, not *vice versa*, but I still felt that it would feel awkward to have to immerse myself in this strange bath under the supervision of an unknown (and, I assumed, probably judgmental) *"mikvah* lady." I asked my closest friend to come with me, as a witness who represented that part of the Jewish community with which I felt most closely identified.

The *mikvah* turned out to be a very clean, white-tiled, small pool. The *"mikvah* lady" was friendly and helpful. The water was warm and embracing, supporting, not strange. The lady made me dip twice to make sure that not even one hair went unimmersed. Then I repeated the blessings out loud so that the rabbis, who were standing outside the door, could hear.

I did not feel born again, nor did I feel cleansed. But I did feel that I had done something important, that it had helped me reach a new level in a spiritual journey that would last the rest of my life. As time passes, I appreciate the *mikvah* even more. It marked an important transition.

Rabbi Wolfe Kelman, who supervised my conversion, suggested that I invite my friends and family to an evening service at our synagogue in which I would participate. It was a wonderful idea because I could immediately do something significant to begin my life as a Jew. I had learned a passage from *K'riat Sh'ma,* which I led, and I learned to read one of the evening prayers. I also gave a short talk about my conversion. I wanted my mother and sister to hear that my decision grew out of my love for them, and I wanted my friends to understand more about my decision.

> To me, this is a very important moment, a moment of passage, but one that is part of a continuum. I used to think that conversion meant that you stopped being one thing in order to become something different, and for that reason I resisted it. But Adin Steinsaltz gave me a more organic metaphor. Conversion, he said, is like marriage. You are joined to a new community, but you bring to the union the strength and values that have been your foundation throughout your life. My conversion, for me, marks officially a love that I've already experienced deeply.
>
> That love began as the respect which my parents taught me for Jewish people, as the commitment which they instilled in me to

speak out against racisim and anti-Semitism. My sisters, Connie
and Peggy, and my brother Richard, have always shared that
commitment. I was moved last year when my mother asked Paul
and me for books to read about Israel for, she said, "I have Jew-
ish grandchildren, and they need a country where they'll always
be safe."

I fell in love with Paul seventeen years ago. Over time I have felt
my identification with the Jewish people broaden from him to his
parents Polly and Lou, his brother Geoff and his sisters Holly
and Liza, to my friends here tonight, to the larger community
and the country Israel. It became increasingly important to me
not simply to identify with Judaism, but to become a Jew. I've
always been proud to be a Yankee from New England. Now I'm
proud to be a Jew as well.

Finally, I'd like to talk about two of my most important teachers,
Lisa and Matthew. Of course Paul and I have tried to influence
their values and beliefs by sharing with them our ideas, our fam-
ily histories—Midwestern Jewish and New England Protestant—
and by creating places for them to learn: the Purple Circle Day
Care and the *Havurah* School. Our families and friends have also
shared much with them. But we have also learned from them.
They have shown us what they see as right and wrong, fair and
unfair, important and trivial. I respect their opinions enormously.

Today marks an important step for me, a step in the search we all
share to lead lives that are meaningful to ourselves and useful to
others. I feel strengthened in that search by my children, my hus-
band, my parents and siblings, and by my friends. I also feel
strengthened by affirming publicly that an important part of the
person I strive to be is being a Jew.

After the service, everyone came over to the house for a pot-
luck supper. I made sure to include my non-Jewish friends, and
my many Jewish friends who didn't think conversion was nec-
essary for me to be a part of their lives, as well as my religious
Jewish friends who were very happy that I had chosen to be-
come Jewish.

It took a while after I officially became Jewish to feel Jewish. People in our synagogue were extremely accepting of me. I actually began to work there as program director a few months after my conversion. But just as born Jews often have difficulties in defining what being Jewish means to them, I, too, had a lot of growing to do. For a long time, I had been aware of not being Jewish. Now when people made remarks that I didn't look Jewish it took months until I was comfortable in saying to them that many Jews look different these days. When people referred casually to *shiksas* or to *goyim,* or said that a Jew by choice isn't really Jewish, I was not comfortable at first in pointing out the prejudice or insensitivity beneath such remarks.

Gradually my Jewish identity has grown stronger and stronger. On the first anniversary of my conversion, Paul bought me a corsage. Now I have trouble remembering how many years I have been Jewish because it seems like always. And this year, for the first time, I felt no loneliness at Christmas. We go every year to visit my sister for the holiday and each year I had felt a little sad that my kids don't "own" that holiday the way I did, and I felt a sense of separation from my sister. This year, though, I felt totally at peace with my decision. It was wonderful to be with her and her family, to share in their joy, but to realize that I had found other riches.

I have found a way of life that incorporates daily, weekly, and yearly observances, that has its own rich cycle, that meets my needs for tradition, for ceremony, for community, and for God. As I grow as a Jew, I also grow as a person. What separates me as a Jew makes me a stronger, more caring, patient person, better able to work with all kinds of people, and to work with them to make a world that is better for all of us.

Closing Words

THIS book has sought to introduce you to a vast and sometimes complex subject: Judaism. Each topic dealt with deserves book-length treatment. (Some topics require several books!) I have restrained myself from expanding and elaborating because I did not want this introduction to be unwieldy. There is more to Judaism and Jewish life than can be covered in one book.

There are some subjects that I have omitted. One such subject is literature. I would have loved to include poems and excerpts from fiction and essays, stories, novels. I also had to forgo a presentation of Hebrew, Yiddish, Ladino, and other tongues dear to and developed by Jews. I deeply regret being unable to present a discussion of some contemporary issues in light of Jewish tradition.

Unfortunately, there are many Jews who do not know much about the subjects presented in this book. They may have memories of pious parents and grandparents; they may have attended a religious school in their preteen years or even until confirmation; they may have been members of a Jewish youth group. But the knowledge, which was neither extensive nor intensive when first acquired, faded as the years passed. As a result, converts often know more and observe more than those who were born into the Jewish people.

Such people have been in the back of my mind even while I was consciously addressing those in the process of becoming Jews. My personal goal has always been to persuade people to learn about Judaism, to convince Jews that they should make their decisions based upon Jewish tradition, to inform non-Jews that they will better understand their own religion and Western civilization if they learn the basic teachings of Judaism. Unfortunately, in high schools and universities, Western civilization is traced to its Greek and Roman roots but its Jewish roots are ignored.

There is no proselytizing note in this work. We Jews do not claim to possess the sole truth; we do not assert that non-Jews are mistaken or doomed or sinful. To be sure, we seek understanding and mutual respect. And those, we are convinced, require knowledge.

Whatever your reasons for wanting to understand the essentials of Judaism, we want to help you gain that comprehension and we hope that this volume has been helpful. A passage in the Mishnah discusses a number of practices for which there is no prescribed limit. They include respect for parents, acts of lovingkindness, and restoring peace between one person and another. This Mishnah concludes: *Vetalmud Torah k'neged kulam*, "the study of Torah is the most basic of them all." In a later generation, that conclusion was questioned. Why should "study of Torah" be more important than honoring father and mother, giving charity, and performing good deeds? The answer given: Through study, one learns what to do and how to act.

I hope that this book will lead you to understanding and that the understanding will lead you to good living, and, for those who are Jewish, to good *Jewish* living. If it accomplishes that, those of us engaged in presenting this work will be richly rewarded.

Index

ABOUT THE AUTHOR

Simcha Kling, ordained by the Jewish Theological Seminary of America, is rabbi of Congregation Adath Jeshurun in Louisville, Kentucky.